MICHAEL J MORRIS

BUSINESS
SUCCESS

Starting a Successful Business

Your guide to setting up your dream start-up, controlling its finances and managing its operations

8TH EDITION

KoganPage

Publisher's note

Every possible effort has been made to ensure that the information contained in this book is accurate at the time of going to press, and the publishers and author cannot accept responsibility for any errors or omissions, however caused. No responsibility for loss or damage occasioned to any person acting, or refraining from action, as a result of the material in this publication can be accepted by the editor, the publisher or the author.

First published by Kogan Page in 1985
Second edition 1989
Third edition 1996
Fourth edition 2001
Fifth edition 2005
Sixth edition 2008
Seventh edition 2011
Eighth edition 2017

120 Pentonville Road	1518 Walnut Street, Suite 1100	4737/23 Ansari Road
London N1 9JN	Philadelphia PA 19102	Daryaganj
United Kingdom	USA	New Delhi 110002
www.koganpage.com		India

© Michael Morris, 1985, 1989, 1996, 2001, 2005, 2008, 2011, 2017

The right of Michael Morris to be identified as the author of this work has been asserted by him in accordance with the Copyright, Designs and Patents Act 1988.

ISBN   978 0 7494 8086 8
E-ISBN 978 0 7494 8087 5

British Library Cataloguing-in-Publication Data

A CIP record for this book is available from the British Library.

Typeset by Integra Software Services, Pondicherry
Print production managed by Jellyfish
Printed and bound by CPI Group (UK) Ltd, Croydon, CR0 4YY

CONTENTS

ACKNOWLEDGEMENTS

Many people have made helpful introductions, others have kindly given their expertise and time to correcting my errors and still more have contributed their first-person accounts of the perils navigated in establishing their own businesses. I hope I have remembered you all in the list below; if not, I apologise. They are:

Melloney Cambell, Ontario, Canada; Barbara Chapman, New Zealand; Oscar Chang, Taiwan; Andrew Chiski, Canada; Rivers Corbett, New Brunswick, Canada; Rachelle Desorcy, Canada; Paula Fernandes, Baltimore, Maryland, USA; Gary Francis, Australia; Jarrod Goldin, Canada; Shanny Hill, Canada; Virginia Kristensen, England; Elliot Leung, Hong Kong; Joanna Lundt, Japan; Scott Mallory, Rhode Island, USA; Karl Martin, Toronto, Canada; Eleanor Morris, England; Tim Morris, Sydney, Australia; David Mulholland, FCO Tokyo; Ken Ng, Malaysia; Nutch Nazeer, Switzerland; Angela Nibbs; Eunice Nyala, Kenya; Pat O'Brien, Republic of Ireland; Jeremy Ouvry, England; Radek Pallach, Poland; Leo Panousakis FCO Athens; Stuart Pohler, England; Mohammad Qayyum, England; Nate Schlachter, Portland, Oregon, USA; Daisuke Shigematsu, Tokyo, Japan; Duncan Smith, star international chef; Santosh Thota, Hyderabad, India; Leonardo Valente, Argentina; Danny Wurr, Switzerland.

In addition I should like to thank OakNorth Bank Ltd for permission to reproduce one of their advertisements.

Finally, I am grateful to my infinitely patient wife, Frances, for her quiet and unstinting support.

Any errors or omissions are, of course, nothing to do with the people mentioned above but are entirely my responsibility.

PREFACE

How to use this book

Unlike other texts, this is really three books in one:

- a conventional textbook, telling you the important things you need to know and do before starting in business;
- a practical manual on how to set up and run a business;
- The PLG Programme © (Prepare, Launch, Grow).

The PLG Programme © helps you to create your plan for investigating the ins and outs of your new business, getting it up and running and, once it is established, making it grow.

New for this eighth edition

In this revised and fully updated eighth edition, fourteen case-studies from around the world feature thumbnail sketches of how recently formed businesses set themselves up. Furthermore, people deeply involved in their foundation offer advice they wish they had been given when they were thinking of setting up. A further case-study is from an experienced South African businessman with much mature advice to share. In addition, there is a new summary of the principles of Islamic banking.

This new material is invaluable advice from people further down the road than the readers of this book, but not so far down as to be out of sight. It is 'from the horse's mouth' advice that is simply not available from any other source.

Starting a Successful Business is already the classic book of its kind. For over 30 years it has helped a whole generation of entrepreneurs to get going with maximum effectiveness. This new edition brings it all up to date and adds extra features.

Good luck!

Michael Morris

First thoughts and foundations

THIS CHAPTER COVERS

- being a business owner-manager;
- family and social life;
- personality, experience and success;
- family finances;
- types of business;
- IT.

What's your big idea?

Every successful business is powered by a big idea – even if it's only a small firm. It comes before the product, the market, the premises, the staff, the money or anything else. (Those things are vitally important, of course, and we come to them later in great detail, but it helps a lot if you first develop a big idea to drive your company.)

Consider a religious or political movement; the whole point of a religion or a political party is that it puts forward a big idea, in these cases a picture of future bliss, either in an afterlife or here on earth. The human need to believe in some meaning beyond mundane daily existence makes such ideas the most potent commodity known to man. They are responsible for all the political and social revolutions that have ever taken place, for the way that we live our lives and for the way we bring up our children.

Tap into the strength of the big idea, and you harness a surge of power that can carry a business on to worldwide recognition. Consider what I see as the big ideas behind these great businesses:

- John Lewis Partnership: if the staff own and run the company, they really care;
- Apple: powerful IT made relevant and easy, presented in beautiful forms;
- Mercedes-Benz: utmost performance and reliability enjoyed amidst comfort.

Two of these firms started some generations ago, but in one, a member of the original founding team ran it until recently what drives them, and drives their public appeal, is not the product itself, but the big idea behind it.

There is no government control on ideas, no exam you have to pass, no licence you have to buy – to power your business with a big idea all you have to do is to think, to project your mind into that of the customer, to think what that person really wants. And then to put it into action, in every aspect of your operations. Make everything you do, say, write or make fully consistent with that big idea.

That consistency is important. Suppose your big idea is to make the best-engineered kitchens in the world: the finest design, the best materials and made to the closest tolerances. Think of the customer who buys your kitchen, then finds it is installed by ill-mannered people who mess up her home and run weeks over schedule. It's not enough to do one part of the job well – *the whole of the customer's experience* has to be consistent with your big idea. That runs well beyond installation, to after-sales service and even a phone call a few weeks before the guarantee expires to see if there are any niggles to be sorted out.

What could be the consequences? For a small firm that intends only ever to service a local market, that business should become a permanent fixture that everyone flocks to, which scares off thoughtful potential competitors who realize that they could never compete, and flattens the foolish ones who dare to try. For a firm whose operations are scalable, it could lead to national or even global standing.

Scalability

Some firms are limited to being one-person operations, simply because there are few, if any, benefits to be gained from making them grow. Example: a domestic window-cleaner. The costs of entry are low (basic equipment, simple marketing) and the only market resistance comes from people happy with their present arrangements. The service is provided by the business owner, with all that implies for quality, responsiveness and low overheads. What could a multi-employee firm offer instead? They would stand a chance only where there was a shortage of window-cleaners. They might get some business, whereupon the staff doing the work would quickly see their chance, resign and offer the service themselves. Thus the multi-employee firm would quickly fail. The only way it could work would be in offering a total glass-cleaning service to firms with large or multiple premises, where a number of staff and expensive special equipment would be needed because of the size or dispersal of the job.

On the other hand, many businesses are scalable, that is to say they can be built up from one member of staff to several, dozens or far more. A precision engineer might start with a couple of CNC machines that he alone operates, acquiring more and more (plus the staff to go with them) as he gains more and bigger customers and ending up with an empire in which he wears a suit and tie all day and spends half of his time out of the country.

Many, many types of business are scalable – but if your ambition is to get big, be sure that you go into the sort of business that can grow, not one that will prove to be a dead end.

What governs scalability? Basically, as the firm grows there must be disproportionate gains from occupying more or bigger premises, buying more materials and supplies, employing more people, shipping greater quantities or having more or bigger customers. If your firm cannot show at least one of those, and preferably more, do not expect to make it grow significantly.

Take the example of one world-famous designer. (Her PR people have asked me not to name her.) You might think that she could work on only one project at a time, which would severely limit her ability to expand the business. To improve her income she might decide to keep the firm at its original small size, but charging higher and higher fees as her reputation increased. She decided differently, and as a result now has sales of over £15m and employs 30 people.

So how does it work? She handled the problem of scaling up her business by being deeply involved with each project at the start and at the finish. She makes the sale and takes the client's brief, then hands the task over to her staff to work up into a finished state. Once that's done, she checks it all for quality, tweaks it if necessary and returns to the client to sell the finished project. Between the start and the finish she keeps a close eye on progress but – and this is the key – does little of the design work herself, and instead supervises the work of others. Meanwhile, she is off working on the next client pitch. The formula has worked pretty well, allowing what could have remained a one-woman business to scale up to quite a respectable size.

The big idea doesn't have to be complicated – indeed, it's probably best if it is simple. Think of the example of the West End shirtmaker T M Lewin, who had a single shop in the 1970s and grew in 30 years to 85 branches, plus a thriving mail-order and web-based side. Rather than selling an individual shirt for around £30, they packaged four together for £100. Customers often felt confused about choosing between a number of attractive styles, and the package gave them permission to spoil themselves and buy several instead of one or two. By that simple idea, the average sale rose from something over £30 to close to £100, a huge leap.

The big idea can come about just by observing the constant swirl of events. Outsourcing has created innumerable opportunities for experts in some business process or activity to set up their own outsourcing operations. Again, the move to cloud computing (discussed later in more detail) means that immense computing power is available to anyone. Instead of having to buy, house and maintain servers, anyone with an IT-intensive activity can simply rent time on someone else's equipment. This change means that where a decade ago only very rich individuals or big corporations could contemplate running an IT-intensive business, now anyone can do it. However, to know what the opportunities might be, one needs to keep up to date with what is going on. A good, general business newspaper (such as the *Financial Times*) will report the facts, leaving you to work out the implications and do further, specialized digging.

Lucky, lucky you!

In business, as in life, luck can play a great part in one's fortunes. To some extent, it depends what you mean by 'luck'. Many entrepreneurs tell of talking to the person in the next seat on a plane, thus meeting their biggest customer, or of their job being made redundant at exactly the moment when they'd written their business plan. However, there is a strong case for belief that you make your own luck, summed up in Thomas Jefferson's saying: "the harder I work the luckier I get".

Professor Richard Wiseman of the University of Hertfordshire has researched what makes people lucky. His conclusion is that what really counts is your approach to life. He puts forward four principles to ensure good luck:

- Expect good luck: that alone often makes it turn up, not through some mystical force of wishful thinking but by creating a receptive frame of mind.
- Create opportunities, notice them and act on them.
- Trust your gut feelings about people and situations, act on hunches.
- When bad things happen, think about how much worse they could have been and think of ways to tackle them.

I would suggest a rider to that final point. When bad things happen, analyse what caused them, think of how they could have been avoided and – above all – learn from the situation. With luck, you'll make sure it doesn't happen again.

Be a master, not The Apprentice

For some years a TV programme has run a competition, the prize being the chance to become an assistant to a well-known businessman. There is a danger that some people, unacquainted with business life, might imagine that what they see on their screens reflects the real thing. It is a game show, not a documentary, so it is important to remember three things:

- the programme's main aim is to entertain, not to inform;
- game-show contestants are not necessarily selected for their ability: their potential to provide entertainment comes first. The more bizarre the behaviour, the more it is seen as entertaining;
- the vast majority of business operations involve long-term cooperation and collaboration, not trying to knock one's contemporaries off their perches so as to leave you the last one standing.

What is my qualification for saying this? Certainly, I don't have the multi-million-pound fortune of the show's leading character. He is an exceptional individual of great accomplishments, but most people are not, and could not be, like him. Some, myself included, would not want to be.

As a more ordinary individual with less distinguished achievements, I do have a lifetime of experience at levels that most people could identify with. Moreover, I have spent quite a lot of time working with entrepreneurs and studying how they go about things. I cannot think of one who would have excelled on any sort of TV game show – instead, they got on with building what are, in many cases, sound and respectable businesses founded on respect for customers, suppliers and staff. That is the sort of business which this book proposes.

What's it like to run a business?

In a word, busy. There is a lot to do and, in the early days, probably only you to do it.

It can be managed, though, and the key word is 'managed'. Most of the really effective managers use three tools:

- the priority matrix;
- Pareto analysis;
- time targets.

All of these tools aim to do one simple thing: ensure that you use your time to best advantage. Take the example of two people of reasonable intelligence and education who live to the same age. Over their lives they get exactly the same allowance of time, yet one may be highly successful, the other not. What makes the difference? The answer is: **how they put their time to use.**

The priority matrix

Everything you do, or don't do, can be put into one of the four boxes on this diagram:

Figure 1.1   The priority matrix

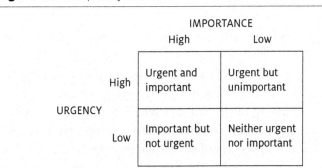

The message is clear. There is never enough time to do everything, so train yourself to:

1 look at each e-mail, letter, phone call or visitor;

2 stop for a split second to place it in the correct box on the matrix;

3 deal with them accordingly.

This way you get all the important things done. You may even do nothing at all from the bottom right-hand box, at least until they have migrated to another box, but a lot will just sit there and fade away. No problem: deal with them once they migrate, but not before. You will save a lot of time.

Does it really work? Our next tool shows how formidable it can be.

Above all, do not aim for perfection. If you do, you will waste time on trivia – time better spent on important things.

Pareto analysis

The Italian economist Vilfredo Pareto (1848–1923) found that 80 per cent of the wealth in Italy was owned by 20 per cent of the population. From that finding much research was done in many fields, culminating in the '80/20 rule', which states that, in most situations, about 80 per cent of the effects come from about 20 per cent of the causes. In a shop, that means around four-fifths of the sales come from one-fifth of the stock; in a sales force, four-fifths of the business comes from one-fifth of the customers; and in a firm like yours, *four-fifths of your profit will come from one-fifth of your effort.*

Yes, that's right – you'll make most of your week's profit in only a few hours.

So it is perfectly obvious where to focus your time: on the few things that will achieve a lot. Conversely, you will avoid or post-pone the majority of things that earn relatively little.

The message becomes even more stark if you apply the 80/20 rule to the rule itself: 80 per cent of 80 per cent is 64 per cent; 20 per cent of 20 per cent is 4 per cent. This suggests that 64 per cent of your results will come from a mere 4 per cent of your work. Just think what that means: *in a couple of hours you could earn two-thirds of a week's income.*

What do you do with the rest of the time?

You can, of course, take it too far. If Tesco offered little more than pet food, washing-powder, cornflakes and wine, some people with eccentric lifestyles might still shop there, but most would go away.

Figure 1.2   The Pareto Distribution in action

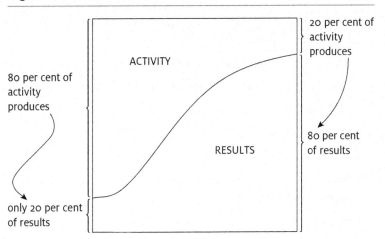

Just as Tesco has to carry lots of slow-moving products, so you will have to do a certain amount of low-profit work. Nonetheless, it is vital to ask yourself two questions: from minute to minute, 'Am I, at this moment, doing the right thing?'; at the start of each day, 'Am I planning to do the right things today?'

And, really importantly, at the end of each day: ' What can I learn about how I spent my time today?'

Family matters

Family does matter: businesspeople need understanding and support from their nearest and dearest. An absent mother, father, spouse or sweetheart tries the patience and dumps responsibilities on others, yet you will still want to be looked after following your difficult day. Moreover, there may be times when money is tight – think what that could do to cherished relationships. So keep them in the picture, listen to their viewpoints and keep them on board.

You, personally, may at first find it hard to come to grips with your new situation. If you are used to long hours, hard work, uncertainty and stress, you have some idea of what is in store. You may need to pick up all sorts of new skills quickly. Ideally you are a person who:

- takes responsibility for your actions;
- has a go at challenges, but assesses risks first;
- is disciplined, sticking to the task even when things get tough;
- understands most of the jobs that will be done in the new firm;
- picks up information quickly;
- has reasonable intelligence and a good memory;
- is imaginative, foreseeing problems before they crop up and getting round them;
- looks for better ways to do things;
- leads, rather than being led;
- keeps clear records;
- can make yourself understood easily;
- gets your own way, pleasantly;
- has good general health;
- really, really wants to succeed.

You find that list demanding? Don't lose heart – it says 'ideally'. Few people get 100 per cent on all of those measures and, in any case, there are short cuts. If your memory is poor, you have probably found ways of keeping notes and filing them; if unimaginative, you can use other people to have bright ideas (there are all sorts of sources of help – see later); if you don't naturally keep records, you can either employ someone who does or discipline yourself to do it. And so on.

If inclined to doubt yourself, think of the generations of immigrants over the past century who came to Britain with nothing, yet built great business empires. Don't you have a head start already?

If worried about failure, reflect on what many tycoons say: that their failures taught them what they needed to know in order to succeed. Failure is a permanent state only if you make it so.

Four types of entrepreneurs

Many people who start businesses fall into one of these categories: craft or technical specialists, managers, salespeople or administrators. Each has strengths and weaknesses.

The craft or technical specialist

Strengths

- Practicality;
- know-how;
- curiosity about how things work;
- creative;
- high standards;
- concern for detail.

Weaknesses

- More interested in things than people;
- undervaluing their work;
- missing the big picture;
- making things better and more expensively than the market wants;
- obsessed with product rather than customers;
- spurning sales skills, believing that good work should speak for itself.

Key challenge

Getting on top of the people skills.

If they team up with someone, that person should have a big vision, perhaps a salesperson.

The manager

Strengths

- Getting things done to deadlines;
- planning;
- dealing with and managing people (some managers, that is);
- vision;
- understanding complexity;
- language, reasoning and numeracy (some managers).

Weaknesses

- Used to an institutional setting where many essential things are done by others;
- unused to doing the detailed dirty work;
- sometimes an inflated sense of personal importance;
- belief that the small firm is just a smaller version of the big firm (whereas it is very different indeed);
- difficulty in switching from institutional to entrepreneurial life.

Key challenge

Making the transition from narrow responsibility to responsibility for everything.

The salesperson

Strengths

- Vision;
- optimism;
- drive;
- persistence;
- people skills.

Weaknesses

- Misplaced self-confidence (sometimes);
- unused to doing the detailed dirty work;
- over-optimism;
- inexperience of the complexity of other functions in the firm;
- making commitments incautiously;
- believing paperwork unnecessary;
- spending heavily on 'front';
- overriding colleagues through force of personality, even when others are right.

Key challenge

To grasp the complexity of the whole business whilst still using sales skills effectively.

A good partner would be a strong-minded administrator.

The administrator

Strengths

- Getting things done to deadlines;
- planning;
- understanding complexity;
- numeracy;
- organization;
- meticulousness;
- keeps records and can access them;
- caution.

Weaknesses

- Over-cautious;
- indecisive;

- narrow vision;
- lacks social confidence;
- lacks people skills.

Key challenge

Broadening vision, developing people skills.
 An ideal partner would be a salesperson.

Women entrepreneurs

Research and experience suggest that, compared to *most* men entering business, *most* women are:

- harder working;
- more careful;
- more accurate;
- more serious;
- more enquiring;
- more likely to admit to inability;
- more likely to seek and listen to advice;
- quieter and less flamboyant;
- less inclined to push themselves forward;
- better at dealing with people;
- more likely to worry;
- more likely to underestimate themselves;
- more likely to blame themselves when things go wrong.

This list generalizes, and people vary, but on the whole I believe it to be true. Lacking confidence, women tend to do more research and seek advice more readily. Being worriers they will think round a situation before committing themselves. Consequently they tend to set their firms up on good foundations. They also tend to keep records and to be good at dealing with customers, suppliers and staff. Sadly, they can also be good at persuading themselves that a perfectly good idea cannot work.

Some women have reported trouble in raising finance. A search under 'funding for female entrepreneurs' brings many hits from a variety of sources. Two of note are Angel Academe and AllBright. The first claims on its website to take seriously women entrepreneurs, and tech start-ups with women on the board (www. angelacademe.com). AllBright go further, specializing exclusively in financing women entrepreneurs (www.allbright.co).

My hope is that sharing these views and reflections will encourage more women to develop the confidence that their ideas and abilities deserve. I write it hoping I have avoided being patronizing.

Male entrepreneurs

Although the gap is closing, men still start more companies than women. In comparison, their firms tend to:

- grow faster;
- get bigger;
- be more ambitious;
- be technically based;
- be faster-moving;
- be better at self-promotion;
- have trouble keeping staff;
- go bust more frequently;
- have more crises on the way.

I leave it to anthropologists and social psychologists to explain why. The sheer fact of numbers means that male-run firms continue, for the moment, to be the backbone of the small business movement.

Thus, any man starting in business would do well to pause in the headlong rush to get going and ponder the comments above on his female counterpart. A more thoughtful approach can pay off, handsomely.

Personal finances: spring clean while you can

As a new entrepreneur, financially you will be close to an untouchable. Until there are three years' accounts to show, nobody will want to lend you money. When raising finance for the firm this need not be a problem, but as a citizen it could be.

Do the following straight away:

- Build into the business plan a reasonable and rising personal income.

- If you are currently in work and plan to buy a house at some time, do it now or postpone the idea for five to seven years (when your accounts will show you have the income to pay the mortgage).

There are some other adjustments to make as well. As an employee you are used to deductions for income tax, National Insurance (NI) and pension contributions. In addition you may be getting subsidies that will be cut off when you are self-employed, including:

- employer's NI contribution, about a tenth of pay;
- employer's pension contribution, a quarter of pay or more;
- paid holidays and bank holidays, another tenth;
- private use of a company vehicle;
- private health insurance;
- life insurance;
- lunch allowances;
- free use of phone, PC, photocopier, unmetered supply of pens, paper, envelopes, Sellotape, Post-Its.

Alone, the first three items on the list total up to 45 per cent of pay. Just because you do not see them does not mean they do not need to be made up in income from your firm. To ignore this point is to fool yourself.

Table 1.1 Main differences: big business employee vs small business owner

Activity	Big company	Small business
Collecting money from customers	Someone else's job (unless you are the credit manager)	Your job, and crucial to survival
Return on investment	Often expect to postpone profit for a year or two, as long as there will be a return eventually	Has to be more or less immediate
Overall management of the firm	The job of some remote figure	Your main job
Attention to a narrow specialism	You are paid to be a specialist	You are a *general* manager now, so keep the specialism in its place
Break-even point	Often at a high level of sales	Needs to be kept as low as possible
Profit margins	Preferably fat, but volume makes up for thin ones	Must be high, because there is little opportunity to go for volume
Raising money	Usually the job of someone else, on behalf of a firm that carries real weight	Your job, backed up by little or no clout
Attention to detail	It pays to have three people working on something affecting 1 per cent of £100 million sales	Deal only with important things. One per cent of your sales in year one is less than £1,000, most likely

(continued)

Table 1.1 (Continued)

Activity	Big company	Small business
Spending 'small' sums of money	£1,000, £2,000 or even £10,000	Spend nothing, if possible; if not, spend little
Using specialist advisers	On the staff, available free and more or less on demand	Select good ones; be prepared to pay, use wisely and get value for money
Prestige and appearances	Big offices and cars, good furniture and location are vital	Get nothing that doesn't really work hard for you
Delegation and help	People on hand to take on tasks	You do it or it doesn't get done
Complete understanding of objectives	A few people at the top, with big problems of communicating them more widely	Possible for every employee to have it
Responsibility for going broke	Shareholders and directors	Yours

This is only a selection of some of the main differences between running a small firm and working for a big one. Not all large companies have the slightly muddled attitudes that may be suggested, by any means. But, despite the shake-out of recent years, many still do. The table does point to the considerable change in attitude that the big-firm manager must undergo to adjust successfully, build on strengths, and survive.

The practical implication is clear. When planning your finances, require the business to pay what you need to live on, plus half as much again, to make up for the lost 45 per cent.

What sort of firm to start?

This question is understandable, but is about as useful as asking what sort of child to have. Whatever the firm starts as, it is quite likely to evolve with the passage of time as new opportunities arise and are explored.

Success stories include people who stuck to a field they knew, as well as those who broke away into something completely novel. The only really sound advice that applies to everyone is this: take time to investigate every aspect before committing yourself. Never again do I want to meet people like the couple who, having taken early retirement because of the wife's health, took out a big loan and sank their savings into a hotel. Only once they had started did they realize it required from each of them 18 hours' work a day, much of it physical, seven days a week.

Even so, it is possible to come to a decision. If you have not already decided what to do, try these as starting points:

- knowledge of an industry, looking for unsuspected opportunities in a field you know;
- knowledge of a sport, game or pastime, seeking ways to supply others with that interest profitably;
- knowledge of an occupation or profession, supplying erstwhile colleagues with some service they need;
- looking at things for sale on eBay, seeing what strange opportunities exist to sell almost anything;
- if you have contacts in retail or manufacturing, buying cheaply ends of ranges and seconds;
- getting a job in an SME (small or medium-sized enterprise) and learning how they work;
- noting the frustrations of everyday life – what could be done better, and designing a business that does it.

If you conclude that you have no useful knowledge at all, check that belief with someone used to thinking creatively and laterally. It might be a family member, someone in the pub or a business adviser; the important thing is to free the mental logjam.

Unless there are very good reasons to the contrary, do not just copy on a small scale a former employer. If that was a manufacturer, you might be able to supply the market without making a thing, perhaps by linking up with a subcontractor or even an overseas supplier, relieving you of a great deal of trouble.

A talk to the commercial attachés of other countries or even a trip out there could yield all kinds of opportunities to import or to act as sales agent in the United Kingdom.

These thoughts lead on to another, one of general principle. Which do you feel more comfortable with, the idea of dipping a toe in the water at first and building things up if it seems to work, or right from the start committing to doing the full job? In many types of business either is possible. Equally, you may feel that anything short of full-blooded commitment guarantees failure.

Those are questions of temperament as much as judgement and you need to think out the answer for yourself, best of all with advice from someone who knows you well.

It is worth forming a relationship with a business adviser so as to have someone to bounce your ideas off. This must be someone with a fine balance between imagination and realism as well as experience outside a narrow, professional field.

Buying a business

Just as with used cars, there is a reason for the vendor to sell. It might be innocent or it might not. Two thousand years ago the Romans used to say *caveat emptor* (let the buyer beware), still sound advice today.

As with starting a business, buying an existing enterprise calls for deep and thorough investigation. If you are unfamiliar with the type of business concerned, ask to shadow the vendor for a week.

That is how you will discover things you would not have suspected. For example, running a village shop might look restful, but how will your back stand up to shifting several tons of stock a week? That is a van-load lifted off the cash-and-carry shelves on to a trolley, off the trolley to the van, out of the van into the store and out of the store on to the shelves. Every week.

Thanks to the supermarkets a large proportion of small shops are under threat – not just the grocers. Look at the growing range of goods they sell and ask yourself: 'How could I compete with this?' If you can think of a way, go ahead, but if not, be careful. Online traders can pose a similar threat. For example, most medium-sized towns are lucky if they have a single photographic shop. The reason is plain: people try out the £300 camera in-store, then buy it online for a little over £200.

Does the business depend on the involvement of the seller – does it virtually cease to exist without them? What is to stop them selling to you, then opening up again down the street? Your solicitor would ensure there was a clause in the sale agreement to stop that particular trick, but you are potentially open to every form of human knavery.

When buying a business you are expected to pay for:

- any freehold or unexpired leasehold, which is reasonably easy to value independently;

- any machines, vehicles or equipment, again easily valued independently;

- stock, usually 'at valuation', a major source of trouble since the valuer might in haste not notice that the stack of boxes is hollow or that the liquid stock long ago dried out;

- 'goodwill', which is a payment for expected future profits: since it is based on assumed future earnings it can be highly contentious.

If you think it appropriate, try to get a clause in the sale contract to commit the seller to consultancy for three or six months, so that you have someone to turn to for information over anything puzzling you.

Taking up a franchise

The uncertainties of starting your own enterprise and the risks of buying an existing business can cause people to think of franchising. A franchise is a (usually) proven idea that is already running, offering the reassurance of an established model.

In a nutshell, you pay the franchisor a sum of anything from a few thousand to over a million pounds, sign an agreement to buy your supplies from them and observe certain standards, hire some premises and get to work. In return the franchisor usually offers national publicity and advertising support together with plentiful business advice. There may even be a loan scheme. As far as the public is concerned, you are just the local branch of an (inter-) national concern.

Many highly respectable firms offer franchises and there is an annual fair at which many exhibit.

You might ask:

- Do I need to buy a franchise to get into this business, or could I do it off my own bat?

- Am I the right person for this?

- What is the turnover of franchisees and why is this particular one available?

- Do they want a high fee up front and low continuing payments? Is this suspicious?

- What is their record?

- Can I finance it, especially if sales turn out worse than they project?

- Have I evaluated this as carefully as I would my own business idea?

Talk to the banks (some employ franchising specialists), advisory agencies and the British Franchise Association (**www.thebfa.org**). Get your solicitor to explain the full range of your responsibilities under the agreement. Because this option has so many special characteristics, it is covered in more detail in Appendix 5.

Example
1

South Africa

A businessman of great experience operating in South Africa – let's call him Peter, which is nothing like his real name – is happy to offer his advice to new entrepreneurs, but asks to remain anonymous.

Peter's advice to the new entrepreneur is firstly to attend to funding. 'Finding the balance between institutional and equity funding at the onset is never going to be easy. Start-ups, in my opinion, tend to give away too much equity and control at the outset.' So the message is that, if you have to relinquish equity at all, be as miserly as possible, and always retain at least 51 per cent. The short-term solution to the start-up's funding needs can lead to a very short honeymoon which is followed by long-term rancour as shareholders of near-equal power jostle to impose their ideas.

Such an imbalance of power between shareholders can lead to trouble later: 'SMEs are best run by one shareholder. If I was just CEO and not also controlling shareholder, then I'm sure that I would have been fired at least every two years. It's not possible for two or more people to always have the same expectations and commitment.' But the picture isn't all negative by any means. 'One of the biggest advantages of an SME is that it can make long-term bets. Big corporates have to feed a steady flow of profits and CEOs are seldom in their jobs for longer than five or six years. They need to keep picking the low-lying fruit to survive. An SME can go without profit growth for years whilst it puts down foundations and invests in the future. As long as your family are fed and the banks and creditors get paid you can carry on.'

He also has advice about publicity, which he believes applies in any country. 'The more public one is, the more scrutiny one attracts. It's not that we have anything to hide, but public exposure doesn't always lead to an accurate picture. It's rather like inviting the Revenue to do an audit: no matter how clean your books are they will always pin something on you.' (The experience of drafting this text bears out his point. My first draft got hold of the wrong end of the stick entirely and misrepresented his meaning. Mercifully, I checked – but one cannot rely on time-pressured journalists to do the same.)

For Peter, then, the SME is able to look to the long term, a great competitive advantage against bigger rivals who need almost to consume today's harvest to remain in business tomorrow.

Starting a green business

The opportunities for new businesses that take account of environmental concerns are many. Consumers and organizations seem keen to reduce waste and their carbon footprints; governments announce almost weekly new initiatives designed to boost the sector. The UK's changing relationship with the EU may alter its regulatory regime, which may spell opportunity for some. It is such a recent change that it presents both special risks and special opportunities: both are covered at greater length in Appendix 6.

Your IT strategy

Every firm needs to record data, analyse it to create information and communicate. In all but the very smallest, information technology (IT) is needed.

The minimum that most businesses have is:

- accounting software (approved by HM Revenue & Customs, or your VAT submissions might not accepted);
- a spreadsheet for budgeting, costing and 'what if?' exercises;
- word processing, for correspondence and documentation;
- e-mail;
- a reliable broadband connection;
- sound maintenance arrangements that react quickly to any problems;
- a printer/copier/scanner.

They may also have specialized software suitable for a specific type of business.

Getting equipped ought not to be haphazard, but planned along organised lines:

- Specify your current and likely future requirements (not the equipment, just what you want it to do).
- Select the operating systems and software.
- Decide if you will ever need a LAN (local area network, to link more than one terminal).
- Specify costings and the programme for implementation.
- Consider the impact of implementation on the main business and have contingency plans ready in case of delay or failure.

You may need advice from an adviser skilled in this area. It is best if he or she is independent of suppliers.

Use of IT for web marketing applications is discussed elsewhere, but it may also have a role in keeping suppliers, staff and associates in touch. When people wanted to update associates they used to send out a letter; now, increasingly, they put it on the website and social media.

There is an alternative to owning your own IT system, by becoming part of 'The Cloud'. Under the traditional arrangement, the firm owns, leases or rents its computing power and applications software and takes responsibility for network security and maintenance. Under cloud computing (CC), the firm creates the software applications it needs, but then places them on a server that sits somewhere else on the globe, with a simple terminal connecting to it via the telephone line. All the complexity of maintaining IT hardware is removed at one sweep; instead of owning the means of IT, the firm rents an all-in service. At the same time it is not using some centrally provided software but creating its own, which it then places on the CC server. A major advantage is said to be the ease of recovery from some catastrophe: a small firm whose PCs are stolen and which has not done its data backup is crippled, probably to the point of collapse. Conversely, if the data are held not locally but somewhere else, the loss of terminals is a small matter as the data themselves are still safe and untouched. A new terminal and a telephone socket put the firm back in business.

Superficially it may seem that CC is ideal for the smaller user, and such may prove to be the case. The big firm can justify having in-house arrangements as the costs are spread over so many PCs, laptops, notebooks and other items of equipment. Yet even there, as firms pare back their operations to the core activity, outsourcing what they do not strictly need to do themselves, CC is growing in popularity. Whether it is right for the new firm, whose start-up requirements may amount to no more than a PC and a laptop, is likely to depend on its likely rate of growth. It may be worth paying over the odds at first, secure in the belief that the basic systems are in place so that growth can take place smoothly. Possessing its own equipment implies occasional upheavals imposed by the need for leaps forward in systems development. As the CC market develops and competition intensifies we could quite possibly see packages aimed at one-person firms and even individuals.

All this is fine, so long as the internet and the CC provider remain viable. What happens if some disaster, natural or man-made, overtakes the internet or the remote server farm is not entirely clear. For those interested, the following is a useful survey of CC services: uk.pcmag.com/mailchimp/82335/feature/the-30-best-cloud-services-for-smbs-of-2016. (SMBs is the US term for SMEs.)

Web trading

In the last few years the internet has changed almost everything in business. Almost, because however good electronic communications become, the world will still needs people to do the final bit of practical work to finish the job. You might order your new carpet, bath or loft-ladder online, but it will have to be delivered via a business running a white van, and installed by a carpet-layer, plumber or joiner. Or perhaps, in due course, a robotic 3D printer, delivered by an autonomous drone – but those days may be some way off.

Thus, while the internet has undoubtedly changed the environment for every business, and has undoubtedly enhanced what practical people can do, it has not made huge changes to the nature of practical work itself. The house extension may be drawn by a CAD program, the engine fault diagnosed by a black box or the structural stresses calculated at the touch of a button, but measuring-tapes, spanners and saws still need to be wielded by skilled human beings. As a result, there are today practical people setting up businesses as they always have done. Whilst some net-based activities have made aspects of their work easier, if the internet had collapsed yesterday they would still be working today.

At the same time, there is a vast range of businesses now thriving which, only a decade or two ago, were scarcely even imagined. All depend for their existence on the internet, and operate in very different ways from what they might call Business 1.0, the way the commercial world has run since time out of mind: people buying and selling between individuals and companies.

So today we now have, running in parallel, two very different models of how business is done. Business 1.0 will always be with us and will probably continue to be tied more or less to the fortunes of the wider economy. On the other hand, Business 2.0, the internet-based variety, has already expanded explosively, worldwide – and continues to expand. Sticking a metaphorical pin in the world and landing on Singapore, then looking at a list of its start-ups displayed on one random day, showed that 19 out of the first 20 depended entirely for the internet on their existence.

There has always been attrition among start-ups: according to some studies, as many as eight out of ten fail in their first five years. 'Fail' is not always the right word, as in many cases people learn lessons from their first business model, which they discover is going nowhere, and then use that experience to launch a new version that, they believe, will work. Perhaps, for those, 'withdraw and remodel' would be a better expression than 'fail'.

There are grounds for suspecting that during this current manic phase of the development of web-based commerce we will see both more, and more rapid, failures and much quicker expansions. Why? For two reasons: first, immediate exposure to most of the people on the planet gives near-instantaneous feedback on how an offer is seen by the market – if an offer is unpromising it can be seen quite quickly, so that it can be withdrawn and either killed off or remodelled within a short space of time; and second, having the entire world as a market means that a good idea catches on very fast globally and its growth-curve can be almost vertical.

Yet sceptics will rightly ask if, from the viewpoint of the entrepreneurs concerned, the differences are really that great. After all, the B2.0 firm still has to persuade people to buy which, for non-trivial expenditures requires contact between two or more human beings, just like the farmer wholesaling flowers to florists from his new polytunnel. Trivial expenditures can be automated completely – if a purchaser finds that the 79p App she just bought isn't as good as she'd hoped, she'll shrug, delete it and move on. But the software company charging a major supermarket tens of thousands of pounds for a suite of programs to control a delivery fleet won't find anyone buying off-the-shelf. Instead they will need to attend many meetings with numerous personnel before getting agreement. Just like the firm that sells them their lorries, in fact, following a model that has existed, in the case of motor transport, for around 100 years.

So perhaps the firm selling trivial items, like our App developer, is much the same as the long-established business operating drinks machines. The merchandise is put on display, some people buy, most don't. If you get a poor drink you might complain, but many people would put it down to experience and simply not use that machine again.

And perhaps our software developer selling to industry has more in common with the lorry supplier than he might think. Both have to stimulate enquiries, follow-up sales leads and demonstrate a superior fit to the customer's needs, as well as to undertake to fix any problems arising from the purchase. And like all businesses, they each have to keep more cash coming in than is going out.

The fundamentals of web trading are identical to those of any other form of selling. There must be a *proposition relevant to the customer*, at a *suitable price* and available on the *right timescale*. The business must generate cash faster than it absorbs it, and preferably make a profit.

Typing almost anything into a search engine produces enormous numbers of links to websites that want to sell something. Should you follow their example of how to go about it, or not? There are so many that this is an impossible question to answer. What I can do is to commend two companies with which I have had dealings and for which I have great admiration. For the record, I know nothing of them apart from as a customer, they are not paying me for this and I have not even sought their permission to mention them:

- www.smallbattery.company.org.uk: The high street shop wanted £15 for a replacement phone battery. The web threw up several promising-looking contacts. All except one needed further information before committing to supply me, so I ordered from the one that simply gave me a price around £16. It came two days later, but wouldn't fit. I rang (unlike many web-based operations they gave a phone number) and it turned out that I had ordered the wrong battery. The right one arrived next day and MailOrderBatteries is now my first port of call for batteries. I hope that my purchases never make them rich, but I think they have the right formula.

- The Map Shop: I wanted Netherlands maps that showed cycle paths. Again, more than one supplier turned up but the online information was not quite what I needed. I rang the name I knew, a big firm, but they put me in a queue. Then I dialled The Map Shop. The woman I spoke to immediately recognised my problem, knew the answers and told me what I needed. The maps even arrived the next day.

In both cases they have the web-trading fundamentals right, but back them up with authoritative phone support. They understand the customer, know their field and deliver satisfaction. The web is not propping up a fundamentally weak business model; rather, it is projecting a sound model widely, indeed globally.

The lessons I draw are:

- Any niche is worth exploring, even if it looks crowded already.
- Add extra value for the customer and you can brush even large competitors aside.

- Dissatisfaction with an existing service can spark off ideas for a new business.

- *The total service is what matters*, not just the website.

Starting an internet business

The phenomenal rise in internet trading, with plenty more potential yet to come, leads money to go straight to this option. While adding an internet dimension to a conventional business is discussed on page 58, here we look at a purely web-based business.

For the time being, all projections for web-based sales are strongly upward. People are increasingly short of time, and those most time-poor are often cash-rich – by working long hours they earn well, and so can pay to have things delivered, which is just as well as they do not have the time to visit the shops themselves. The extraordinary success of Ocado and other home-delivery retailers is testament to that. Yet it is not a new idea – 50 years ago every small grocer had a delivery boy, who collected orders from customers' homes and delivered the merchandise (and the bill) later that day or the next.

One barrier to entry has been swept away by recent developments. No longer is there a need for an intimate understanding of web-page programming: contractors have always been available, but, since many now specialize in the small-business market, costs are now affordable at a few hundred pounds upwards. Alternatively, it can be done really cheaply, using the various free tools that the internet offers. One website of many that give both an excellent overview of the process, and detailed instructions on how to do the entire thing free, is **www.website setup.org**. Professionally designed, a website should cost between £1000 and £4000. There are many packages; free and paid for.

Another model is to sell via eBay or Amazon, who offer a range of packages to would-be traders. It is not for everyone, but many an individual has developed a lucrative sideline or even a full-time business by selling (and sometimes buying) there. Both offer monthly subscripiton services at various levels and Amazon will even gift wrap and deliver if required.

Attracting the customer

Internet-based trading has developed to the point at which it is now quite normal to deal with a business that has no physical presence, being represented solely by a website. That, in turn, has brought a number of new concerns for customers. Some websites act as if a low price is the sole consideration driving buying decisions. That may be true for a proportion of customers, just as there are people who will happily buy goods from a stranger in a pub car park, sight unseen, for cash. Sometimes everything is all right, but for many people's taste such a transaction leaves too much to chance: the more cautious will prefer to pay a little more in order to get some assurance of service if there should be a problem.

A customer who finds a website that admits to no physical address is immediately on guard. Some forms list under 'contact us' their physical address, telephone and e-mail contacts; others omit all of this, using just a form to enable the customer to speak to them. In the latter case, if the seller declines to respond, there is no possibility of the customer taking some problem up. Not all customers are stupid enough not to realize this, so the website that overlooks it appears suspect and puts itself at a disadvantage.

Website design

What the homepage looks like obviously matters; especially to be avoided is too much text. It is important not to go too far the other way, with all kinds of bells and whistles that slow down loading (customers are impatient, and a slow load will have them going off elsewhere). Things to avoid include:

- over-elaborate content;
- video;
- visual effects (flashing effects, animations, etc).

Typeface for text should recognize that not everyone's eyesight is perfect. If your customer profile is elderly, this is especially important. Navigation needs to be straightforward. The FAQs (frequently asked questions) should be comprehensive, covering all conceivable problems and thus cutting down on the number of queries that come in for personal attention.

'Contact us' should incorporate an enquiry form, rather than just an e-mail address hyperlink that will open Outlook Express, which is not everyone's preferred e-mail editor, and takes time to load.

Where there is a lot of information to cover, break it up under separate headings and devote a page to each – rather than creating one or more pages of dense text.

'About us' on many websites is sometimes boastful, saying too much, sometimes bashful, telling too little. The happy medium is to tell the story of the business briefly but with enough detail to make its founders and other key staff seem human photos help a lot here.

Keeping customers happy

Customers, and the satisfaction of their needs, lie at the heart of any proper business, so it is worth spending a moment considering some of the relevant issues. Anyone who has bought from the internet will be familiar with the trader who offers low prices and quick delivery, takes your money and then reports that they are briefly out of stock. Only after a week or two, when it dawns on you that they had no stock in the first place, do you start to chase them in earnest. If you have spent £100 or more and have bought with a credit card, you will get your money back if the delivery never turns up, but for lesser purchases the customer is unprotected.

To pontificate, it should not be part of any business plan to behave so shoddily. Quite apart from the morality – the seller has no right to take money for goods they cannot supply – there is the practical matter of reputation. Satisfied customers are said to tell five people; dissatisfied customers, 20. But wrong is not always on the part of the seller, so wise vendors protect themselves from unjustified claims of non-delivery by use of one of the signed-for services. Part of the FAQs section should be answers to questions about what to do if things go wrong, either with the delivery or after the sale is complete.

It must always be remembered that, although a web-based firm may have many characteristics different from those of its conventional equivalent, it is identical in one simple respect: it makes its living only by pleasing its customers.

Consequently, it is also well-advised to follow the guidance elsewhere in this book. Selling on the internet does not confer immunity from the eternal truths of business.

Less glamorous matters

As has already been hinted at, designing and operating the website and getting the order is only part of the job. Processing of payments and fulfilment of those orders accurately and in the time promised is crucially important. Systems should be set up to ensure that all this takes place, and they should be tested (even if only on paper) to see if they can cope with extreme conditions.

If your product has a physical presence, storage, handling and delivery need to be planned for.

Finally, like running a pub, operating a web-based business is a 365-day-a-year commitment. How will it run while you are sick or on holiday?

CASE STUDY Bugs will save the human race

Whereas farmers regard many insects as pests bent on consuming the crops they are struggling to raise, for Entomo Farms of Canada, insects *are* the crop.

Based on a philosophy that the world's current system of agriculture is not sustainable, the three Goldin brothers set out to create human foods from the most prolific protein source that the planet supports, creatures with six legs. They use the term 'geoentomarians' to describe people who will intentionally choose to eat insect-based foods as a contribution towards saving the planet. As far as they are concerned, the movement is well under way, with more than two billion people worldwide already incorporating insect protein in their diets. All that remains is to persuade the rest of us to follow, and especially those of us in the developed world.

There is something almost evangelical in their work. As Jarrod Goldin says: 'It's no longer a fringe view that many of the world's ecosystems are close to collapse, but mainstream. Scientists accept that animal and human diets need to change radically. We simply can't go on with resource-intensive arable and livestock production the way we have done.'

Fortunately, he says, insects represent a far more sustainable food-source, and they are plentiful. Whilst there is debate around it, some religious authorities have declared them both kosher and halal. Entomo's crickets are raised organically and claimed to be virtually gluten-free in their normal form, with a fully gluten-free version also on offer. Only people with shellfish allergies need to take any precautions, they say. In return, the foods contain many health-giving elements in more concentrated form than in most intensively-raised components of the Western diet.

There is no shortage of species to choose from. According to the UN's Food and Agriculture Organization, 1462 types of insects can be eaten by humans. Among them are crickets (similar to grasshoppers), which themselves come in 900 varieties. Whilst they can be, and are, farmed in dustbins, the Goldins' commitment to work with nature drove them to create specially-designed accommodation that mimics their native habitats as closely as possible.

'What we do is simple,' explains Jarrod. 'Once the crickets approach the end of their six-week lives they are humanely harvested, roasted and packaged, or are ground into flour for use in cooking. Our website gives many recipe suggestions showing the versatility of the product and thus, we hope, increasing uptake.' In addition, they sell roasted mealworms, a larval stage of a beetle, which has been eaten by humans since time out of mind. They add a nutritious crunch to salads, soups and sandwiches.

Entomo Farms also supplies livestock farmers with products that they believe are much more cost-effective than other forms of protein feed. That side of the business is being taken forward through collaboration with university researchers in animal nutrition. But they aren't stopping there, as further work goes on towards the therapeutic use of the products.

Entomo distributes through direct sales from the website as well as through wholesalers to retailers. Trade is international as they sell to distributors in a number of overseas markets. This is a business that has done a number of clever things. It has inverted the farmer's usual relationship with insects, applied a visionary zeal springing from personal convictions that they share with a growing number of people to creating a market virtually from scratch and has identified a low-cost, short-cycle source of the bulk protein that the world badly needs. Quite a story.

Website: entomofarms.com

Key jobs to do

- Understand that the firm's success largely depends on how you use time.
- Ensure that your family understands and accepts the implications of your decision.
- Assess your strengths and weaknesses in relation to running a business.
- Set your personal finances straight.
- Decide on the type of firm to start.
- Recognize that if you are ever going to pull out, now is the best time – though you might find it useful to finish this book first.

Getting orders, making profits

What are you selling, exactly?

Your job is to sell what customers want. If it is an innovation, they may not know they want it, yet. But even within the realm of what they know, different customers want different things. Think of reasons why people might buy clothes:

- warmth;
- weatherproofing;
- lightness;
- fashion;

- allure;
- long life;
- versatility;
- good service;
- quick delivery;
- … and so on.

No clothing supplier could satisfy all those needs, which is why different suppliers address different segments of the market. It also prompts the thought of injecting ideas from one category into another – making functional clothing fashionable, for example. One of your first jobs is to identify the segment(s) you are aiming at, then sell to it or them.

Sometimes the buyer is buying for himself or herself, sometimes not; sometimes the decision is influenced by others. You may need to reach those others, too. Think about who takes the decision to buy from these suppliers:

- Building contractor – householder or architect?
- Toymaker – child, parent, grandparent, other relative or friend?
- Subcontract precision engineer – engineering designer or engineering buyer?
- Security software developer – security manager, IT manager or CEO?

Do those different audiences want to hear the same message from the supplier? How is it in your chosen trade?

Look carefully at your market, ask around, investigate; find out how people buy in the area where you plan to operate and gear your proposition accordingly.

Choosing customers

First, define the end-user of your product, your consumer, the person who ultimately gets to use it. Think of how they get the product now. Conventional ways of reaching them may work for you, but perhaps other routes are possible. Are there any other ways it could get to them? Are any of them practical?

What does your consumer really need? It may be that they are not getting it, or not in full. Could you supply the missing element?

Often those two pieces of thinking specify a possible new business: the product can be the same as others, but it gets to consumers in a way they prefer and with add-ons that they like.

Think of John D Rockefeller, who gave away oil lamps; he soon got his money back through the boost to his sales of paraffin. Or Kodak, whose early cameras were sold at cost in order to shift film. And Gillette, who did much the same with razors. They all broke the rules that everyone had assumed existed up to then, and none of them died poor.

To address consumers effectively, they need to be grouped together into market segments. There are many bases for segmentation, including:

- geography;
- age group;
- how much of the product they use;
- income group;
- social class;
- leisure interests;
- … and so on.

For example, a lawnmower repairer and retailer might decide to segment his market using a number of criteria:

- within 30 minutes' drive, to concentrate his effort;
- owner-occupiers, assuming that tenants might care less about their gardens;
- landlords, on the same reasoning;
- 50 to 1,500 square metres of lawn, as smaller lawns may be mown by cheap, throwaway machines and larger by contractors;
- in small towns, villages or suburbs, as lawns are scarce in cities;
- purchaser size;

- geographical location;
- number of branches;
- number of staff per location;
- or any other measure relevant to what they are selling.

By doing that they have done two key things: decided who they will concentrate on, and decided who they will ignore. Both help them to maximize the return for their efforts. Do the same for your business and your marketing will be more effective for it. The opposite, aiming a scattergun at all possible targets, guarantees wasted effort.

Finding out what you need to know

So far we have assumed that you either know what you need to know or can easily lay hands on it. Even if you do, the time will come when you need to do research. But where to look?

Internet searches are an obvious starting point. One good place is **www.rba.co.uk**, which provides a number of lists, some useful to business.

If you are a B2B seller, you may at first need little more than **www. yell.com**. It lists all the 1.6 million *Yellow Pages* entries and enables searches by geographical area as well as business type. So if you want to sell to UK accident investigators (they have 65) right through to zoos (87), you can list your sales prospects instantly and for free.

Information on the web is not always reliable, though, and some that is, is costly. At some point you may wish to visit your local public library. The commercial and reference section (all the bigger libraries have one) is staffed by people who know their way around the information scene. They also subscribe to the important directories, both paid-for online and physical books so that you have free access.

Often, the challenge lies in knowing where to look. Ask yourself who else has contact with the people you want to talk to. For example, to sell B2B locally, try asking for lists from:

- local authority estates department – who are their tenants?
- local authority promotion units – what businesses exist in the area?

- Chambers of Commerce – membership directory;
- Chamber of Trade – ditto;
- trade associations – membership lists;
- business clubs – membership lists;
- colleges – local employers.

Not all will help, but some will, so ask. More widely, there are government development agencies, government websites, national trade associations, industry directories and web-based lists. You can also tour industrial estates on Google StreetView, spotting sales opportunities from a comfortable chair.

The more specialized your target group, the more likely there are to be societies, websites and magazines to serve it. Some even commission research among their members which may tell you exactly what you want to know.

Forecasting your sales

At the outset, there are three possible approaches to sales forecasting:

- decide it is impossible and don't bother;
- make a forecast based on cautious realism arising from research;
- forecast sales at a level that you think looks realistic and will at least pay the bills.

Either of the second two is fine, depending on your circumstances. A blend of the two may be even better. The first is not. All the financial planning for a firm starts from its sales forecast, so don't shirk, but do one.

Forecasting Demystified

Many people refuse to make a forecast on the grounds that it is bound to be wrong. They are right: it is. But that is no reason not to make one.

So why spend time and trouble on something that will be wrong? Because *accuracy* isn't the point. You try to get it as right as you can, of course, but being 5 or even 10 per cent adrift does not matter a jot, as long as you spot the deviation early and correct for it.

The case for forecasting is compelling. Running a firm is a complex game, with many variables impacting on each other. The owner needs to keep on top of the game, and the best way so far devised is to make a forecast, then see how things turn out. If the forecast is wrong, you change it. In changing it you also change all the variables that depend on it, which provides a new set of benchmarks against which to measure progress.

It is a bit like riding a bicycle: you proceed in a series of swerves, never a straight line, but always in the general direction of the objective.

If you did not have the forecast, how would you know what the objective is?

If you don't know what the objective is, how do you know which direction to go in?

From the sales forecast you will know:

- how big the production facility needs to be;
- the production capacity required;
- how many staff to take on;
- what transport capacity is necessary;
- your cash needs;
- how much material to order;
- seasonal peaks and troughs;
- … and so on.

Understandably, the new business founder can feel intimidated by this task. Uncertainty and ignorance are the problems. Cut down on the unknown area by visiting some potential customers and simply ask what you need to know. Explain it is a research visit and avoid all temptation to sell, but listen, really listen, to what is said.

Even then you may lack the knowledge to have sufficient confidence to take the plunge full-time. Could you start up part-time? Could someone else make what you supply until you are confident enough to go in for the big investment yourself?

This discussion is closely linked to the 'Breaking through to profitability' section (in Chapter 3), which looks at the minimum level of sales needed to pay the costs, which is the point where you start to earn profits.

What exactly *are* you selling, then?

Customers do not buy products or services. Customers buy propositions. The total proposition is much more than the mere product or service. If that were untrue, Marks and Spencer would never sell another shirt, for shirts are available from market stalls at a third of M&S prices.

Compared to the market trader, M&S offers:

- a quality-controlled product;
- self-selection;
- protective packaging;
- authoritative advice if needed;
- a guarantee of performance;
- instant, no-quibble exchange or refund;
- payment by credit card;
- a pleasant, clean, indoor environment.

The shirt itself, plus all of that list, comprises the M&S proposition to its customers. Yet M&S do not have a monopoly. Why?

M&S aims at the middle 60 per cent, leaving 20 per cent at either end for others to pick up. They are the people who want either something much fancier or much cheaper, or easier parking out-of-town, or the convenience of a retailer near their workplace, or to buy at home by mail order or on the web. Those other suppliers have their place, providing what *their* customers want, at a profit.

Work up your proposition, looking at every aspect of the way the customer might view it. Above all, remember that not all the people who make it big invent a better mousetrap. Many attach other benefits to perfectly ordinary mousetraps, which is a lot easier than inventing improvements to a design that already works perfectly well.

With that in mind, whether or not your product truly is a revolutionary leap forward, look at all the variables that you can change: response to enquiry, order size, delivery speed, guarantee, servicing, spares, after-sales follow-up and others. If you can be better at any of those in ways that matter to your customer, you should win the business.

Whenever you are in doubt about a course of action, it helps to draw up a table showing the pros and cons. Here I have made one to help you assess how different patterns of delivery could affect your competitiveness against the opposition.

Making this sort of examination of every aspect of your plans against what the competitors do helps you to:

Table 2.1   Delivery competitiveness matrix

Factor	Competitor does it	What we could do	Customer benefits	Our costs
Deliveries	monthly	monthly	none	same as competition
		weekly	lower stocks, more responsive	higher?
		daily	lower stocks, much more responsive	much higher?
	weekly	daily	as above	higher?
		two-hourly	as above	much higher?
		monthly	lower prices	lower

- see how high your competitors have set the bar;
- carve out a specification for exactly how you run your firm;
- once you have been running for a time, review why you do it that way.

The importance of doing this is that most customers assume that what is on offer now is all that will ever be on offer. You do not want to fall into the same trap. You want to lead, not follow, if at all possible.

Probably the most important aspect of your proposition is the benefits that your products and services offer. There are two kinds of benefits: those arising from something built into the thing itself (like a self-sharpening feature on a knife) or those separate from it but still part of the proposition (like a warranty). These are some of the possibilities (the two sides of the table are not meant to correspond with each other):

Built-in benefit	Outside benefit
better-looking materials	faster delivery
more resistant finish	longer guarantee
better performance	no-quibble replacement
needs less maintenance, more reliable	free replacement while servicing done
lasts longer	easy-payment terms

You can ring the changes on column 2 far more easily than on column 1. Thus this is the area on which you concentrate when planning promotional support to give customers reasons for buying now, not next month or next year.

Do not overlook the importance of this. Because the outside benefits are easier to see, they are more real to the customer. That is why an inferior mousetrap in an excellent package will often outsell its better-performing competitor.

Why should anyone buy from you?

Customers buy because:

- your marketing is better, meaning that you have put together a proposition that is more relevant to them than anything else on offer; and
- your selling is effective.

And that's it.

Get this right, and you could be on the way to a fortune. Get it wrong, and there is no point in going any further. Instead, keep working on the proposition until it is right.

But the job does not end there. Competitors could copy your approach and neutralize your advantage; if they do, you need to know. So keep your eyes and ears open and, best of all, have your next two moves up your sleeve ready for immediate use when needed.

Take a look at your firm from the point of view of a customer. What sort of image does it present? Since, in the early days, you and the firm are one, much of the answer will revolve around your personal appearance and presentation. However, there is more to it than that.

Unless you are a skilled designer, don't try to mock up your logo, letter-heading and other documents on the PC. Give the job to a professional who will take what you are trying to put across to your customer and translate it into graphic design. He or she will also ensure that the design is carried over into all aspects of your contacts: business cards, website, letterheads, invoices, quotations, compliments slips, vehicle livery, company uniforms, sales presentation materials, advertising and even the typeface used for correspondence. It all matters. It will cost a few hundred pounds, but could lift you above the crowd.

Once won, customers will keep on coming back provided you keep your promises (some people under-promise so as to be able to over-deliver) for as long as your proposition remains relevant. Their needs will change, so you need to change with them. To allow for the fact that some will stop buying through a change of policy or, indeed, closing down, you need to keep on recruiting new customers all the time.

Getting it all to the consumer

At the two extremes, you can deal either direct with the consumer, the end-user, or through a chain of distribution that ends with the consumer. There are different routes from you to them, each with its own benefits and drawbacks. Selling direct gets you the full sales price but takes time, costs money and involves a good deal of admin. On the other hand, selling through distributors relieves you of a lot of admin but at the price of giving you a lower income per unit. Which is best? It depends on you, your market and the strategy you are putting together. Among the issues are these:

- Who has the whip hand, the salesperson or the producer? (Ask who wins: the salesperson who withholds the order, with the threat of placing it elsewhere, or the maker who withholds delivery threatening to sell it elsewhere?)
- Who would be best at selling for you – you or someone else?
- Which makes more money – selling or making?
- If you dropped selling or making, what would it cost to get someone else to fill the gap?
- If you drop selling, how will you maintain an independent view of what is happening among customers?

We are assuming that there is a realistic option of finding a sales agent, which might not be the case.

The main tangible distribution channels

Retailers are the shops we are all familiar with, of course, together with retailers running web-based shops on eBay and Amazon.

Wholesalers or **distributors** buy from suppliers and sell to independent shops. Occasionally they sell some specialized goods to larger retailers. They usually specialize in a particular sector, eg hardware, pet goods, giftware, etc. They may operate **cash-and-carry** outlets or make deliveries.

Sales representatives (reps) draw salary and expenses and are employed to sell to customers.

Sales agents are independent, self-employed reps working on commission only, usually between 10 and 20 per cent of sales. They meet their own expenses. Try **www.themaa.co.uk**.

Multiples or **chains** are shops with several, or more, branches, often with regional or national coverage. They may have a central warehouse or take deliveries direct to branches.

Mail-order catalogues are big catalogues like that of Argos or Littlewords. Other than Argos, their main consumer proposition is that goods are available on credit.

(Many specialists operate mail-order catalogues to sell their own merchandise. It is a route open to any firm, but here we deal solely with the large, general catalogue operators. Running one's own catalogue is dealt with separately.)

If you choose to use a channel of distribution external to your firm do the maximum amount of research possible before going ahead.

You may decide to do the selling yourself after all. If so, make sure you learn from each encounter, whether you get an order or not. Keep records and analyse them, as you would if you were employing someone.

If you get more than about one order from each four pitches your proposition is being received well, and you might be able to cut back on some expensive element of it, or to raise prices. You can try out different propositions, to see what effect it has on the number of orders you take as well as on profits. Like a good scientist, change only one variable at a time otherwise you won't know which change made the difference.

Dealing direct with the public

The usual methods of reaching the public direct are:

- Website: see later sections.

- Selling in the home: like Avon. To reduce the customer's right to cancel, make sure you are invited in other than on a first visit. Drop a leaflet for them to ring you and make an appointment from that.

- Mail order: in response to either an ad or a catalogue that you send.

- Direct mail: leaflets through letter boxes or letters through the mail. Newsagents will deliver leaflets in small areas, Royal Mail anywhere you like (and cheaply).

- Stalls: in markets, at fairs, shows and car boot sales.

- Party plan: as used by Neal's Yard, Ann Summers and others.

- Showroom or shop.

- Mobile showroom: a converted trailer or caravan, taken to the customer or events where the customer will be present.

- Piggyback leaflets: eg a catalogue for seat covers placed in every new car.

There are more – just look around and every time you see someone trying to sell, ask: how could that be made to work for me?

If you want to sell direct as well as through the shops, be aware that shopkeepers will resist. Use another trading name and address for your direct sales to give the appearance of just another web retailer. If you want to advertise before many shops have taken on stock, say in the ad 'Available from good chemists (or whoever) or from the manufacturer'. That gives you a let-out for selling direct.

A website or mail-order ad offers certain advantages and disadvantages:

For	Against
direct communication with user	pay for ads with no guarantee of results
no dealer to pay	
usually cash with order	at mercy of press circulations
can reach many consumers	at mercy of Royal Mail prices
fast, even in minority-interest markets	at mercy of Royal Mail and press unions
can turn demand on or off by adjusting advertising expenditure	results sometimes unpredictable
reaches consumers that other methods miss	
can operate from home	
over time, builds up a mailing list	
convenient to almost all purchasers	

It applies to all sectors of business and works best where a clearly defined segment is addressed, such as anglers, plumbers or local authority planning officers. All have their own trade press and specialist websites. There are also in some national newspapers pages devoted to ads for mail order. Those ads can be for 'off the page' sales (where the customer orders from the ad) or can invite people to ring for a catalogue.

If you sell off the page, look at **www.shopspromise.com** to see if you have to conform to SHOPS, the Safe Home Ordering Protection Scheme, before your ad will be accepted.

Display ads average about 1 to 2 per cent response from the readership (readerships are available from newspapers' and magazines' websites). A display ad is where you pay for space, rather than a lineage (pronounced line-age) ad which is charged per line.

Equally, a small ad can aim to do no more than stimulate enquiries for catalogues or brochures.

Check whether your business falls within the requirements of the Consumer Contracts Regulations, 2013 or the Consumer Rights Act 2015. Information on those and other regulations is on **www. oft.gov.uk/Business**. The Citizens' Advice Bureau and *Which?* also offer summaries of consumers' rights under legislation, useful for gaining an overview.

Direct mail is another route direct to the customer. Lists of people with almost any interest under the sun can be bought, or, if you operate only locally, *Yellow Pages* or **www.yell.com** may yield all you need, free. To buy lists, go to the big magazine publishers' websites or search for Mailing List Brokers. The Royal Mail publishes a lot of advice to would-be direct mailers, as well as offering a delivery service to postboxes by postcode area.

Designing direct-mail materials is highly specialized. One of the masters is Laithwaite's, the wine merchant. Another is Donald Russell, the Scottish mail-order butcher. To see what good mailings look like, get on their mailing lists. The quality of their work should persuade most businesses that they would benefit from using a specialist copywriter.

Before sending any mailing, check with the Mailing Preference Scheme (**www.corporate.mpsonline.org.uk**) as it is unlawful to send unsolicited mail to anyone who has registered not to receive it. The same organization covers the Telephone Preference Scheme, should you wish to sell by telephone.

Party plan works best for businesses with items to sell at up to £100 or so. You need to recruit hostesses (they usually are women) who invite their friends to their homes using invitations that you provide. You demonstrate and sell, paying the hostess a commission on sales. People already running party plan may tell you the names of hostesses, as they are keen to see good hostesses kept fresh by running parties for a variety of goods. The Direct Sales Association (**www.dsa.org.uk**) might be able to help.

Everyone who attends gets a free gift and it is usual to supply the hostess with wine for her guests. Guests order at the party and either pay there and then for later delivery or place a deposit, paying the balance on delivery.

You get the full retail price, in cash, with only a small promotional outlay. You build up a mailing list for future business (include a tick-box on the order form to allow you to mail them) and may find that some customers are happy to become hostesses.

You will need to operate in pairs so that one person deals with the customers and the other with necessary toing and froing.

Shops' and distributors' margins

Some people become incensed when they learn how much retailers add to their cost prices to produce their selling price. It is a waste of energy, akin to complaining about the weather. My advice is just to accept it and get on with the important things.

Most trades have conventions on what margin they add, based on the speed of turnover, perishability (physical or of style), cost of premises and other overheads and risk. They vary widely. A small grocer might take 7p out of a tin of beans retailing for 69p, or 10 per cent; a greengrocer, 30p in every pound; a Bond Street fashion shop 70p in every pound or even more.

When discussing the profit taken by the distributor one needs to be aware of the specific terms commonly employed and how they are sometimes misunderstood and misused. The terms 'gross margin', 'gross profit', 'margin' and 'mark-up' are used interchangeably, but they mean quite different things. Table 2.2 shows how.

To avoid the potential for confusion, ask each person you discuss this with to take you through the simple calculation of a selling-price, starting with a cost-price to them of £1, £10 or £100. You will quickly see what each of them means by the terms they use.

On a point of detail, the product in the table would be unlikely to be priced at £18.00. Instead, the shop will think of either £17.95 or £17.99. They will want to keep their existing margins, so what difference does that make to the supplier's price? Obviously it cannot remain at £10.00. Taking £17.95 as the example, it drops to £9.97, as shown in Table 2.3.

Once you know the way the retailer calculates prices, you can work out what was paid for anything in the shop. Using the example in Table 2.2, this is how you do it:

Table 2.2 How shops calculate their selling price 1

Cost to shop	£10.00	
Shop adds 50 per cent of its cost	£5.00	This is a 'mark-up' of 50 per cent on cost; 'margin' or 'gross margin' of $33\frac{1}{3}$ per cent on selling price excluding VAT. It is also a 'margin', 'gross margin', 'gross profit' or 'mark-up' of £5
Shop's selling price excluding VAT	£15.00	Usually worked out separately as VAT doesn't give profit to the shop
VAT at 20 per cent	£3.00	
Price to public	£18.00	The price tag in the window

Table 2.3 How shops calculate their selling price 2

Cost to shop	£9.97	(e)
Shop adds 50 per cent of its cost	£4.99	(d)
Shop's selling price excluding VAT	£14.96	(c)
VAT at 20 per cent	£2.99	(b)
Price to public	£17.95	(a)

$c = a \div 1.2$ (or divide by 1.15 if VAT is at 15 per cent and so on)

$b = a - c$

$\quad = c \times 0.2$ (or multiply by 0.15 if VAT is at 15 per cent and so on)

$d = c \times \dfrac{50}{150}$ (or $c \times \dfrac{m}{100 + m}$, where m = the percentage mark-up on cost price)

$e = c - d$

Attracting the distributor

Distributors, shopkeepers included, would like everything they stock to be:

- demanded by customers without prompting;
- exclusive to them, at least in the immediate area;

- not affected by season or fashion;
- unlikely to spoil in storage;
- difficult to steal;
- compact and easy to handle;
- faultlessly reliable;
- cheaper than competitive goods.

Shopkeepers would also like the company supplying them to:

- keep plenty of stock of all varieties, colours, sizes, etc;
- have an instant delivery system;
- offer high profit margins;
- give plenty of support through free display material, display stands, heavy advertising that mentions them by name, contribution to advertising costs, and incentive bonuses that require little effort to win;
- offer unlimited credit;
- be entirely dependable and honest in all its dealings;
- … and a lot more besides.

Most retailers are not fools. They know that there is something wrong with things that are too cheap. So, unless you have a real advantage that enables you to undercut competitors, do not try. Especially, do not start a price war, for the longer-established firm is usually better placed to win. Remember, too, that a fall in prices means a reduction in distributors' incomes, unless it is compensated for by an increase in the quantity sold. What the distributor truly seeks is merchandise that is easy to sell and keeps customers happy.

If your product needs a lot of selling by the distributor, see if you can get packaging and display material to do that job, for shop staff rarely sell anything. Nonetheless, ask the buyer if you might take a few moments of sales staff time to explain the product and answer any questions. Take a look round the shops, builders' merchants and other distributors to pick up ideas and see how other firms tackle the problems of selling through display. Marketing advisers from advisory agencies might be useful here, and elsewhere, too.

If your distributor has a sales force, as most wholesalers do, try to get a slot to present to their next sales force meeting. Stick strictly to the time they allow and you may stand a chance of being noticed among their 4,000 or so other lines. You may want to discuss with the buyer a temporary sales force incentive scheme to get the product going.

Some may ask for sale or return (SOR). This means you placing the goods with them and being paid only if they sell. Ask yourself: which will they try to sell first, goods the shop has paid for or those it has not? Which goods will be kept in good condition, those paid for or those on SOR? Even if you agree to SOR, expect disputes and damage when you come back weeks or months later to collect the unsold goods. If SOR is mentioned, make it clear that your policies do not offer it and get back to selling the advantages of your proposition.

As with any other type of customer, attracting the distributor is only part of the job – holding on to them is important too, accomplished by good service, never being a problem and always listening and looking for new ways to help them to sell your product.

Visiting the customer

Previously you have reviewed the information and illustrations you need to take with you and browsed the shelves of a commercial stationer to find attractive binders to hold and display it. You do not visit buyers at the busiest times: Friday afternoons, market days and weekends.

You have done the research, now you are about to walk in and try to make a sale. You are dressed appropriately, with clean clothes, hands and fingernails, and some attention to personal grooming, including avoiding the use of aftershave and embracing that of antiperspirant-deodorant. (It may seem patronising to mention these matters, but you must meet the buyer's expectations of cleanliness, which may be stratospheric, for all you know.) In your (smart) briefcase you have:

- a note of the absolute lowest price you can afford to sell for, just in case;
- price lists;

- terms and conditions of sale (see Appendix 2);
- order form (or enquiry form if yours is the sort of product that is specially made and quoted for);
- calculator;
- pencils (two, sharpened – a single one always breaks);
- pens (two – one always runs out);
- your laptop or tablet;
- notepad;
- visiting cards;
- diary;
- worked illustrations of selling prices, savings, incentive bonuses, etc;
- photographs;
- samples;
- comparisons with competitors' performance;
- advertising plans and layouts;
- press cuttings;
- display material.

All this should be clean and neatly arranged. One good thing to buy is a loose-leaf ring-binder-cum-clipboard. In the ring binder you can put clear plastic sleeves in which to keep your documents and photographs in the right order, and the clipboard holds order forms and a notepad. They usually have pockets for spare price-lists, customer record cards and so on. Even if most of your materials reside on the laptop, this is a useful back-up in case of battery failure.

If video demonstrations are important, your tablet or laptop will be set up with a DVD or a link to your website.

If a sales rep is already with the buyer, withdraw unobtrusively and wait until their interview is over, or leave and return later.

If the buyer is unavailable, make a note of your proposition on the back of a business card and ask for it to be given to the buyer. Something like: 'Mrs Edwards (are you sure that is the spelling?) – small, low-cost swarf-compactor for machine shops. May I demonstrate, please (3 mins)? John Jones.'

Be pleasant to everyone you meet; you do not yet know who is important. Smile.

If you find yourself in a waiting room with other salespeople, get them to talk about customers you might call on. They are gregarious and often helpful.

Plan the interview itself along the lines of AIDA – see the box.

Smile. Use the person's name – Mr, Mrs or Ms until invited otherwise. In your circle first names may be usual. In the buyer's they might seem over-familiar, so play safe.

The sales interview – AIDA

AIDA is the initial letters of Attention, Interest, Desire, Action. Those are the stages you take the sales interview through.

Questions will feature heavily.

Attention may best be gained by a question: 'If I could show you how to reduce waste by 10 per cent, would you be interested?' That displaces any other thoughts from the person's mind.

Interest is built by demonstration and description of benefits.

Desire may be difficult. We can all think of things that seem interesting but which we do not actually want. It can be developed by showing how much better things would be if they bought. 'From next week you could be enjoying reduced staff absenteeism. How would that feel?'

Action involves placing the order. Do not shrink from asking for the order.

If you get a refusal, don't give up. Seek agreement that your basic proposition is attractive, then ask what the problem is. 'What do I have to do to earn your business?' The answer could be anything from a misunderstanding about the proposition to the need to get someone else's approval. Whatever it is, get back into selling. And keep on selling.

Part of your prior planning will be the sales promotion package: the killer reason you give for buying now rather than later. Promises to buy later are rarely kept. Change the package every time you call, to keep the offer fresh. Over time, the sight of your happy face will inspire in the buyer the thought 'What's this rep got for me this time?' Just by going through the door you will already have got to the 'I' of AIDA.

Ideas you could try include:

- free item (first aid kit?) that you can buy at wholesale price;
- 20 per cent voucher off essential maintenance items;
- £25 rebate for a purchase of two;
- maintenance contract at half price;
- free product with every five bought;
- promotional materials to help their sales;
- ...and so on.

It costs money, of course, but will all be built into your pricing, so there isn't a problem.

Pricing for marketability

The first thing to get clear is the distinction between **price** and **cost**. Price is what you can sell for. Cost is (not surprisingly) what the product or service costs you.

The obvious point is that price has to be at least equal to cost, and preferably it will be higher. Chapter 3 deals with costs.

Competition will limit the extra you can charge over and above cost. That is not to say you have to be cheaper than others, or even to sell at the same price. As discussed, what customers buy is the total proposition, not just the product, and if your proposition looks worth more, you can charge for it.

To put this another way, what customers want is value, not low prices. In some markets, commodity markets in particular, low price matters. Petrol is a case in point. Most people assume supermarket petrol to be good enough, and will shop around for the best offer, thinking all petrol to be the same. However, those in the know believe it worth paying the premium for Shell or BP. They think that the extra price is more than worth it in terms of economy, performance and engine life.

Where you feel you have to compete on price, try setting prices a little higher than the rest. That makes your product look better than theirs. Spend the extra you make on sales promotion activity. This is a trick played in some parts of the motor accessories market. Car wax might have a high list price, which is then reduced by promotional offers. The consumer is invited to think they are getting a superior product for the price of something ordinary. The trade buys the offer, knowing that their customers will buy it.

It is hard to over-emphasize the psychological role of price, in both directions. Something priced higher than the generality must be better. Something priced lower, worse. What people actually pay can be made affordable via promotional offers.

Selling via the big catalogues: big orders, quick payment

In most respects these catalogues are much the same as any other customer. They are open to smaller suppliers but operate in specialized ways.

The buying process runs like this:

- preliminary selection by committee nine months before catalogue launch;
- final selection three months later;
- notification of suppliers and orders for further samples from the successful;
- launch of catalogue;
- repeat orders to suppliers.

They demand completion of many forms and the prediction of prices for the life of the catalogue. All samples you submit for the selections they will return or pay for. The quotation expects transit packaging (be advised by the buyer whether a padded bag or mailing box is needed), but you can take out your normal retail packaging. Guarantees of rapid replenishment will be expected. They will usually pay 50 per cent of their retail price. In return you get fast payment, straight dealing and sometimes big orders.

There is a large number of smaller, specialized catalogues offering all kinds of merchandise, some aimed at the public, others at business. Watch out for them and see if your product could fit in.

Effective advertising

Here we look first at buying advertising space in printed media – newspapers and magazines. Your internet presence is dealt with shortly.

The magazine market is so highly segmented that it is easy to find a suitable advertising medium for almost any proposition. The best source of information on advertising media is BRAD (*British Rate and Data*), which operates by subscription online; some public libraries subscribe. *Willings Press Guide* is next best and all public libraries carry it. The website **www.nrs.co.uk** looks at many aspects of press readership, including the effects of combined print and electronic advertising.

Once you have shortlisted a few titles, look at actual copies in detail. Check that they look like the right setting, and that they do not hide ads like yours away.

Costs of ads can be very negotiable, especially as the copy date approaches and they have empty spaces left to sell. If you can afford to take it or leave it, try a silly offer at the last minute and see what happens. You would not be the first to buy the £1,000 space for £100.

When designing ads, make the benefits the most prominent part of the message.

Always have artwork produced under your own control rather than by the helpful people at the magazine or newspaper. When you get the proofs, check them in fine detail and pick up even the smallest fault, like a spot or a broken letter. Once you have signed them as passed there is no going back.

Once you have become a substantial advertiser (£200,000 a year, say) you should look at small local ad agencies. You could find that they introduce a level of professionalism and give much valuable advice to make the expense worthwhile. In any case, some of their cost will be met by the discount on space given to agencies but not available to you. As always with important suppliers, see more than one and buy only if you feel sure.

Having bought advertising, you will want to know how well it is working for you. To do that you need to know what your aims were before you took this course – exactly what objectives did you have for the ads? If that is clear, and your objectives were SMART (specific, measurable, achievable, relevant and timed), all you have to do is note down the results and compare.

Beware, though, of expecting too much. A manufacturer of equipment for local authorities once told me that advertising doesn't work in his industry. The evidence was that he had placed one ad but no enquirer said they had seen it. Advertising does not work like that. What it can do in that market is deliver messages about you that ensure a warmer reception next time you call. Who can recall which ads they have seen today? Yet be sure, you have been influenced by some of them.

Some advertising terms

Rate card = advertising price list.

Rop = run of paper, ie we put it where we like.

Facing matter = opposite editorial text, not other ads.

Ifc / irc = inside front cover / inside rear cover, plum sites.

Scc = single column centimetre, ie one centimetre deep and one column wide. Ad costs are often quoted per scc.

Litho = lithography, a printing method which makes printing plates photographically, requiring the advertiser to supply 'camera-ready artwork', which most small design studios can accomplish.

Copy date = deadline for receipt of artwork for ads.

Proofs or **pulls** = single sheets printed from the plates for final checking by the advertiser.

Publicity: nearly free and better than advertising

It is a myth that the papers are full of news garnered by energetic and enquiring journalists. Much of the media's content is supplied by organizations keen to get their latest news seen. Even the smallest organization can get in on this free(ish) ride. For the larger operator, **www.cision.co.uk** provides tools to distribute news releases widely.

The mechanism for this very low-cost publicity is the news release. In essence it is a news story, ready-written in journalistic style, which the medium has only to tidy up to match its own policies. If it is too long, they cut it by chopping off the end, so it pays to get the key message across early on. Almost any event in the firm's life can form the basis of a news release; some will be printed, others not, but as it involves no more expense than a stamp or e-mail plus a little time in writing it, most people regard them as value for money.

Publicity is better than advertising in one way: since readers think it has been written by journalists they trust it more. On the other hand, the story can be changed from the interpretation you wanted to one you dislike.

Matters that might trigger a news release could include:

- new firm formed;
- new premises opened;
- business expanding – more jobs;
- new trainee taken on;
- trainee passes exams, gets award;
- big order;
- new products taken on/developed;
- first/hundredth/thousandth order;
- worked overtime/weekends to get job out;
- to show at exhibition;

- results of showing at exhibition;
- first/second/etc anniversary;
- government grant;
- new executive;
- new machine;
- open day.

Don't overlook sending copies to local radio and TV, both BBC and independent.

To write a news release jot down the key points of the story using the journalist's six prompts: who, what, why, when, where and how. Write the story, or get someone to do it for you, with key messages early on. Double-space and print at 10 words per line on one side only. Head it NEWS RELEASE with the date, then the headline and the story. At the end, write ENDS and put a contact address to show it is genuine and a number for further information. The result might look something like the example shown in Figure 2.1.

The example has the word 'immediate' against the date. If you want it held back, for example if there is a risk that the long copy date magazines might send it to the dailies under the same roof, blowing your story prematurely, you would type here EMBARGOED TO 17 JUNE or whatever date you were happy with.

The web and your market

It is a cliché to say that business has been transformed by the internet. Clichés are clichés because they are true. And this cliché is especially true for the small, niche operator.

A small guest house on a remote Hebridean island used to rely on referrals from tourist information centres and advertising. Demand was uncertain and often arose from people stranded by ferry failure. Demand was limited by consumer assumptions that there would be no accommodation on the island, so it was not worth visiting.

Since launching its website it attracts advance bookings from all over the world. The romantic description of the island, its

Figure 2.1   Sample news release

NEWS RELEASE   Immediate: 27 May

New Delicatessen in Midtown

A lifetime's dream will be fulfilled next week when Tom and Sheila Jones open their new delicatessen and village shop for the first time. 'It's a huge step for us,' said former steelworker Tom, 'but we know there's a real demand for quality food in the area. Other places have some of the things a good cook needs, but we've tried to put everything under one roof.'

True to their word, Tom and his wife Sheila have stocked the shop with food from all over the world, as well as special aids for the discerning cook. Redundancy pay and a bank loan helped, as did advice from their accountant. The shop, at 38 High Street, Midtown, opens its doors at 8 o'clock sharp on Monday morning. 'As a working woman myself, I know how annoying it is to find the shops shut when I get out of the office,' said Sheila, 'so we decided to open at 8 am and close at 7 pm every weekday.'

The first of many events planned is a tasting of French wines and cheeses, with no obligation to buy. Others planned for the future include special demonstrations for the Townswomen's Guilds and Women's Institutes.

ENDS

Further information from:
Tom and Sheila Jones, Midtown 987654,
38 High Street, Midtown.

---

bird-watching opportunities, the chance of real peace and quiet plus good food and accommodation have led to a wealth of enquiries and bookings. There are hotlinks to ferry timetables and reservations, so that the visitor can plan the entire trip from their keyboard.

A children's clothing designer produces colourful clothes but her sales were limited to the area she could cover physically. They are expensive and so only a few could afford them. To become more widely known she needed colour brochures, which would have to be renewed every season, but was prevented from reaching the wider market by her inability to afford them.

After investing in her website an amount that would have paid for a single brochure printing, she updates it now with photographs she takes herself. Click-throughs, on which she earns a royalty, take visitors to websites of associated products. Orders are coming in from around the world and she is working on extending the range to sell footwear, accessories and toys so as to provide a total 'look'. She sees her biggest problem now as managing to retain the personal design vision that inspired the company whilst expanding it to exploit the opportunities on offer. In one role she is a designer, in the other a manager.

The web is also a research resource, especially into marketing matters. Competitors and customers helpfully disclose what they are up to and the chance to look for new ideas, worldwide, is unlimited. Governments and trade bodies publish statistics. Research organizations offer the results of their work on different markets.

The sheer quantity of information presents its own challenges for when the monthly trade magazine was the main source of information, keeping up to date was not a problem. Now the alert business has to set up a regular schedule of site visits to stay on the ball.

Sales via the internet

The main options open to a firm are:

- set up a shop within an existing web business – eBay and Amazon are the best-known ones to offer this facility;
- run your own website, confining it to pre-sales information and after-sales queries but offering no means of immediate contact;
- offer a full service covering enquiries, orders and payments.

The cheapest to set up is the first: conversely, it is also the route with the highest running costs per sale. There is no bar to running simultaneously an eBay shop, say, and your own website, so a cautious strategy would be to start off in Amazon or eBay and later launch your own site.

Search-engine optimization: more hits for your site

When a web search is performed, for example by Google, the search engine examines billions of pages of web content and gives its results in a second or two. Partly that is achieved through awesome computing power, partly through the cybernetic equivalent of a quick glance at each page.

That quick glance can be hindered by the type of software used to create the page (easy-to-use page-creation software is nice for the designer but creates tons of code for the engine to search through), by the structure of the site (frames slow things down a lot) and by the text used (which might give meagre clues to the search software).

The first two of these should be checked with the web designer, who should demonstrate familiarity with the issues and say how he or she avoids them.

The last item is related to the text the website owner puts on the screen. It should not only tell the story, but the story should contain a keyword phrase, of the kind that searchers will type into Google, every page or so.

Sites will need at least several keyword phrases. They should be generated by creative thinking as well as reading competitors' websites to identify the keyword phrases they are using. Software is available that, after the event, will analyse hits to see which keyword phrases are working and which not.

Keyword phrases will be of two to four words each in the vocabulary and structure used by the desired enquirers. For example, a heating engineer may talk of thermal efficiency, where a member of the public speaks of fuel saving. Test the list of keyword phrases for relevance by searching on Google to see what they turn up. Get them right and they will put your site in the top few results every time.

The process for starting a website is straightforward:

1 Specify exactly what the site is to do.

2 Design the site to meet the specification.

3 Check legalities (mainly Data Protection Act).

4 Select a domain name (eg **www.yourname.co.uk**).

5 Check on **www.nominet.org.uk** that the name is available.

6 Select an agent to register that name to you.

7 Select a host internet service provider (ISP) or decide to host the site yourself.

8 Create policies and documentation both for internal use and to appear on the site.

9 Set up arrangements for handling incoming queries and fulfilling orders.

10 Set up payment handling (if relevant): if you take cards, banks have tough rules on CNP (customer not present) transactions.

11 Test.

12 Go live.

Look carefully at how your preferred domain name could be read and avoid the problems of the Italian power supplier, the directory of therapists and the list of experts who are said to have come up with **powergenitalia.com, therapistfinder.com** and **expertsexchange.com**.

Design of your website is obviously critical. It must look right, expressing visually what you want to put across. A professional web designer will cost money, but ought to get you into business quickly and reliably. Not all designers are the same; some use software that actively slows a web search, so when selecting a supplier, run a three-stage test:

• Trawl a number of the sites they have already designed to see how fast they open.

• Perform a web search on those sites using the key phrases you might expect an enquirer to use (for a Portsmouth estate agent try 'houses for sale in Portsmouth' and see if they come up in the first 10).

- Ask what the designer does about search-engine optimization (SEO) and how they take it into account.

The results might be surprising and, if so, give you a warning.

The main features of the site should be speed of loading and ease of use, as people switch elsewhere after only a few seconds' wait. Speed up loading by avoiding fancy graphics, sound and video.

Before operations start you will obviously plan for levels of e-mail and phone contact that seem reasonable. You should also have a contingency plan. What will you do if you get five times that level? Could you get the necessary terminals, phone lines and staff quickly? Do you have the space and insurances?

When customers contact you, put a tick-box to permit you to e-mail them with future special offers. Spamming them (sending them promotional e-mails) without permission is bad behaviour and will lose customers. Never sell your address list to other firms: it is a breach of the trust implicit in the relationship.

Getting this process going is easy. Many website designers advertise locally and firms like BT offer fixed-price packages. Some advisory agencies will set you up. Costs for a reasonably sophisticated custom-built site should be between £1,000 and £4,000 to set up, plus maintenance fees.

Here we can give only an outline of a complex topic. A web search for outline advice reveals many useful articles.

Other new media

Would you benefit from a Facebook page? Could you demonstrate your product or service on YouTube?

Lauren Luke did, demonstrating make-up tips. After getting 70,000,000 hits, she launched her own range.

CASE STUDY   Indians aren't cowboys

Santosh Thota, from Hyderabad, India, along with his company's valued first employee Abhinav Chintalacheruvu, has already revolutionized his business in only its first year of operation. Why? Because the original business model didn't work as well as he'd planned, and he saw an opportunity to move it on in a different direction whilst using the same basic technology – a path which he promptly took.

Asked what Feltso does, Santosh replies: 'Social review analytics.' Fortunately for this writer at least, he goes on to explain. 'We use artificial intelligence (AI) to collect, collate and analyse customers' views, gleaned from feedback and reviews. If someone in a company begins to read its many thousands of customer reactions he or she can get only an impressionistic – rather than scientific – idea of customers' concerns. Immediately after that he or she starts to drown in information, and gives up. The sheer quantity of information is more than any human being can process. And there's more coming in all the time.' The problem, then, is one of scale – a firm getting so many reviews that it cannot possibly understand them; yet they must be understood, for buried somewhere in the mass of data is information that could be vitally important. And Feltso's solution? 'What we are doing is to take a torrent of unorganised information, getting AI to do the sophisticated, hard grind of working out what it all means, and presenting to our client a straightforward, easy-to-understand analysis of it all.' And it is sophisticated. Santosh has trained his analytics on over a million customer reviews, with the result that it can now spot fakes (and ignore them) and even interpret statements like 'Wooooooooooow!!!!!'

Many companies provide analytical services, of course. But Santosh believes that Feltso's edge comes from making its analytics specific to an industry. 'That makes sense to the client', he says: 'Just think of trying to understand your views of your car by looking at it as if it was the last meal you had in a restaurant. It just cannot fit.'

Meals eaten outside the home are relevant here, since the restaurant sector was the first that Feltso tailored its product to. It is a highly-competitive sector – established businesses are constantly under attack from new competitors, fashions in food change fast, what was the right location last year can become outmoded next, and customers move around just to get a change of scene. Gross margins can be very high (just think of the few pence-worth of water, milk and coffee grounds in your £3 cup of coffee), so that small swings in demand can make a big difference to the bottom line. It is also a sector in which people are prepared to write reviews, as a glance at TripAdvisor will confirm. Thus it makes a good jumping-off point from which to launch into other business sectors, a task in which Santosh and his team of four are fully engaged with insights that they can turn into actions.

That was not where Feltso started from, though. At the beginning Santosh had envisaged a buiness-to-consumer (B2C) business model, but after a number of hiccups realised that the future lay with business-to-business (B2B). Funding the start-up costs and recruiting serious full-time staff needed big investment, which he secured by finding strategic investors who contribute advice and experience, as well as their money, to making Feltso a success. And success is surely round the corner, for the problem that Santosh has identified and solved is common to vast numbers of businesses across the globe. With the benefit of hindsight, he wishes that he had devoted less time early on to developing the product, and more to finding and building his team. For the immediate future, he and the team are seeking partnerships that will take the business forward to attain its full potential.

Santosh likens his experience so far to climbing a personal Everest. He had this dream which he needed to pursue, but to make it reality he had to leave behind many areas where he felt comfortable and strike out into unexplored territory. He sees the main challenges as mental, physical and financial, and lasting for at least three years, after which he hopes the company will be self-sustaining. Recognising the physical nature of the demands is important, as working too hard and too long, with extra worry and stress, take their toll, Thus being and remaining physically fit is important. The last thing an entrepreneur needs is to have a health breakdown in the middle of establishing the business.

Is it all worth it? 'Most definitely. It always feels good being an entre-preneur since we have definitely taken a different path to solve some of the world's problems more efficiently,' he says. To my mind, the world is lucky to have such people in it.

www.feltso.com

Key jobs to do

- Research and understand your market.

- Select your marketing strategy – exactly what will you sell, to whom, by what means and in what quantities? How will you differ from competitors? Why should people buy from you?

- Develop your promotional strategy – how will customers hear about you?

- Select your sales strategy – how will you get orders?

- Select your distribution strategy – how will orders be executed?

- Develop your pricing policy – what do you charge, what discounts are available and why?

- Build up forecasts of sales volumes that can be used later to calculate the value of sales and the cost of goods sold.

- Develop numerical benchmarks against which you will measure performance.

Controlling the money

Costs and costing

To sell at a profit, businesses need to know their costs. To take a really basic service, like a window-cleaner: what is the cost of providing his service? Vehicle, ladders, wash-leathers and so on are easy to identify. But what share of those and how much of his phone bill should go to each customer? Or his insurance premiums (which can be sizeable) or pension contributions?

Questions like those have prompted the writing of large textbooks. Here we shall use a single, simple method that serves many firms well in their early stages, and for much longer than that if they do not grow. It is known as the absorption method of costing: in summary, it says that for any one job the cost is the total of materials plus overheads plus labour. Simple, as I said.

Absorption Costing System: general principles

To price a product, service or job, you first need to know what it costs. The simpler the costing system, the quicker and easier it is to use. Absorption Costing is ideal for the small operation as it is the simplest of all the systems available.

To use it, there are three easy steps:

- find out what hourly rate ought to be charged for labour and overheads;

- multiply that hourly rate by the actual number of hours used on the job in hand;

- add on the cost of materials.

The answer is the total cost of that job. Once you've got that, you can move on to deciding what to charge.

The system depends on making assumptions and judgements (so it is not precise), but it is close enough for practical purposes. In summary it works like this (further detail appears later, but it is important to get the general idea first):

- Labour: annual payroll costs for yourself and any staff, including NI, pension contributions, health insurance, etc;

- Overheads: two main sources:

  - annual total of all day-to-day running costs (eg rent, rates, insurance, fuel, energy, hire, phones, consumables, etc);

  - a year's depreciation of buildings you own, plus vehicles, tools and equipment owned but not hired. (Calculate these by dividing what they cost to buy by their likely life in years. Example: a £17,000 vehicle that you will sell for £2000 after five years will have cost £15,000 in depreciation. The depreciation is obviously £15,000 ÷ 5 = £3000 a year.)

- Hourly rate: total the above. Divide the total by the number of productive hours you are likely to work in a year. The answer is your hourly charge-out rate in £s.

- Total cost of job: (number of hours taken × £ per hour charge-out rate) + materials.

Shortly we shall look at how much to charge per hour for labour and overheads. In essence, a firm needs to charge enough to pay running costs plus an income for the owner. For example, the cost of a widget might be:

Materials	24
Overheads and wages, 2 hours × £40 an hour	80
Total cost	£104

If all the hours worked on that product are counted, and the hourly rate is right, and they make the number of widgets they forecast, all of their costs will be covered. Simple.

Remember that the cost of something to you is not necessarily what you sell it for. Rather, cost is the lowest price for which you can afford to sell it.

There is an important distinction between types of cost: those that go up and down with the level of sales (eg the cost of materials consumed) and those that do not (eg the rent for premises). Those are known as fixed costs (which are mostly overheads) and are quite distinct from variable costs (which are mostly built into the product or service you sell like the cement used by a concrete slab maker). Makers and menders tend to have quite high variable costs, through the components that they incorporate in their output. Pure service firms, who are, in essence, selling their staff's time, usually find that fixed costs predominate. The effect on profitability is quite different in the two cases. Once they both have sold enough to cover their overheads, the firm with high fixed costs makes money much faster – at that point almost all its income is profit – whereas the other firm finds that only a proportion of every sale is profit, since so much has to go on components.

In the early days, at least, it pays to commit to as few fixed costs as possible and to keep as much as you can variable. It might cost more, since you might be hiring equipment expensively rather than owning it more cheaply, but at the end of the hire your obligations stop; when you own the equipment it can stand idle but still be costing money. Keeping costs variable gives more flexibility as the business evolves. As you gain experience, your confidence in fixing some costs may grow. Examples include buying-in rather than making things yourself, renting or taking out a loan rather than buying outright, and using subcontractors rather than employed staff.

Calculating an hourly rate

First, work out the costs of running your business. At first, several of the figures will be guesses. That isn't a problem. Even a rough guess is better than overlooking a cost. Include:

- rent and rates;
- fuel, light and heat;
- consumables (but not the materials built into each job);
- vehicle running costs (but not purchase cost);
- staff costs;
- the pay you will draw from the firm;
- depreciation.

Exclude the cost of buying things you will keep and use: tools, vehicles, PCs, software, etc. These are capital costs, accounted for via depreciation.

Depreciation is a charge to your costs that reflects the fact that, little by little, you are wearing out capital items (this is how our window cleaner gets the cost of his ladders back). If you buy a machine for £1,000 that will last for four years, you use up £250-worth of it each year until, after four years, it is in your books as valueless. You charge that £250 to each year's accounts as depreciation, and you include it in the current calculation as a cost. (Ignore the fact that in the real world you can probably sell it for something, or may even continue to use it, after the four years.)

Now we move to calculating how many productive hours you work. In new firms people often work 60 or 70 hours a week, but their productive time, the time when they are doing something that a customer will pay for, rarely exceeds 20 or 25 hours. The rest goes on all sorts of ancillary activity, such as paperwork, doing the accounts or organizing supplier, necessary but unpaid for. So you work out your costs on just the *productive* hours.

Taking out holidays, Christmas and sickness, 48 weeks' work a year creates 48 weeks × 25 hours = 1200 productive hours.

Finally, we can now calculate the cost per hour. Suppose you need £40,000 gross (that is, before income tax and NI deductions) to feed, house and clothe the family and the firm incurs running costs of £20,000, it has to earn £60,000 a year. Look at Table 3.1 to see how it comes out.

If your figure looks high, don't reject it. 'High' does not mean high by comparison with the figures used here – they are only an example – but by comparison with what others in your market charge. Find ways to justify the prices it results in, by being reliable and doing good work. Anyone charging less, yourself included, will fail. If you simply can't see how to make it work, pick a different business model or even a different line of business. Before giving up on the project completely, do get a qualified accountant to look at your workings first. He or she might spot a wrinkle you've missed or see an error in your assumptions; you will never know until you ask. Make sure you minimize the effects on your prices by:

- controlling interruptions, so as to increase productive time;
- work intensively, turning out more in an hour than others;
- use modern equipment wisely, for the same reason.

Table 3.1 Working out an hourly charge-out rate [1]

Productive hours	
25 hours a week × 48 weeks a year = **1,200 productive hours a year**	
Overheads to be recovered	
Family income (gross)	£40,000
Business overheads	£20,000
Total	£60,000
Hourly rate to be charged	
£60,000 ÷ 1,200 hours = £50 per hour	

Controls on costing

Given that the figures used in your costing are estimates and predictions, the one certainty about them is that they will be wrong. That is fine, as the one certainty about forecasts is that they will be wrong. The trick is to keep the error to a minimum through constant review.

To make your predicted costs come about in real life, monitor all the assumptions you made and get early warning of things going wrong. If you manage only 20 productive hours and get 45 weeks' work, there are only 900 hours to recover costs from. Either the hourly rate (using the figures above) rises to over £67 (£60,000 ÷ 900 = £60.60) or your income has to fall by £15,000 (£60,000 − (900 × £50) = £15,000). Nasty, and therefore very important that you keep track of the key factors:

- invoiced sales;
- overhead expenses;
- productive hours worked.

For each of them, set up a simple table showing your weekly plan and running total, against which you can write the actual outcome and running total. Table 3.2 shows an example for the first three months of invoiced sales.

Table 3.2   Keeping track of performance

Invoiced sales, Year 1		TARGET £		ACTUAL £	
Month	Week no	Week	Running	Week	Running
Jan	1	–	–		
	2	100	100		
	3	200	300		
	4	200	500		
Feb	5	100	600		
	6	100	700		
	7	150	850		
	8	150	1000		
Mar	9	400	1400		
	10	400	1800		
	11	400	2200		
	12	400	2600		
	13	400	3000		

It shows at a glance whether you are on target, ahead of the game or falling behind. You then have a chance to take corrective action before the warning becomes a crisis.

Taking on an employee reduces the hourly rate, which does not mean you reduce your price, of course. Table 3.3 shows how.

If the simplicities of absorption costing leave you uneasy, another system is discussed later.

Table 3.3 Working out an hourly charge-out rate 2

Productive hours	
17 hours from owner (less than before because supervision takes time, and selling the extra output takes longer)	
33 hours from employee (44-hour week, 75% productive)	
50 hours a week × 48 weeks a year = **2,400 productive hours a year**	
Overheads to be recovered	
Family income	£40,000
Business overheads	£20,000
Employee's cost to you	£20,000
Total	**£80,000**
Hourly rate that could now be charged	
£80,000 ÷ 2,400 hours = £33.33 per hour	
This means that hourly costs have fallen by one-third – a saving that need not be passed on to customers.	

The importance of cash

'Cash' is loose banknotes or money in a current account. It is the only thing that can be used to pay bills. If bills are not paid, creditors foreclose and the business usually shuts.

Consequently cash is the single most important thing in any business; it is the one thing a business owner watches constantly.

Running out of cash is easy. You do it by stopping money from coming in or sending it out too fast. Just try:

- delaying the sending-out of invoices for work done;
- losing notes of what work has been done, or delivery notes for goods sold;

- not chasing customers for payment;
- avoiding opening credit accounts with suppliers;
- going out of your way to pay bills in cash as quickly as possible;
- buying large quantities of materials to get discounts;
- buying equipment and vehicles for cash instead of getting a loan;
- taking on staff who are unable to work fast enough or to quality standards;
- keeping on staff for whom there is not likely to be any work;
- never checking things that you sign for;
- never getting a signature for goods that you deliver;
- laying yourself open to theft;
- taking on prestige premises when they are not necessary;
- buying fancy insurance policies;
- not cultivating the bank manager;
- never planning ahead to foresee your cash needs;
- never recording performance and comparing it with the plan;
- taking a really big order, especially from a slow-paying customer.

On the last item, taking a big order, the problem is that you pay out your cash for materials, labour and overheads but don't get cash back from the customer for maybe several months. Too often, when the cheque arrives, it is the liquidator who pays it into the bank.

Clever cash conservation

Shrewd business people follow some basic principles:

- Orders agree payment terms as well as price, delivery, etc.
- A sale is complete only when payment has been made.
- Bills are paid only when due, never before.
- Credit accounts are opened with suppliers wherever possible.
- Supplies are bought only for immediate needs, even if that means paying more per item.

- Borrow for property and equipment (the easy borrowing); working capital is harder to borrow, so finance it from your own funds.

- Keep only productive staff who are currently needed: you are responsible for the business as a whole, not for each individual employee. Whilst any employer should behave responsibly towards employees it is not the overriding responsibility. The first requirement of all is to keep the firm in business.

- When staff are at work they are working all the time, and for you.

- Run the firm frugally.

- Have good anti-fraud systems in place, including an iron grip on the accounting system.

Forecasting the cash situation

Some people see this as a nuisance, to be avoided if possible. True, just as it is a nuisance to look both ways before crossing a busy road. Remember: *cash is the single most important thing in any business;* it is the one thing a business owner watches constantly.

Watching cash is a four-stage process:

- predicting cash inflows and outflows;

- monitoring what actually happens;

- do it all over again, for ever.

Any serious divergence and you pounce, not resting until you can say why it happened. It is the most important job of all and must not be neglected.

You need to know four things to create a cash-flow forecast:

- what points in time the forecast is for;

- expected flows of cash into the firm;

- expected flows of cash out of the firm;

- the timings of each inflow and outflow.

Looking at each of those in turn:

- Points in time: usually month-ends, though more often when cash is tight.

- Flows in: the money you invest, money invested by others, borrowings, payments from customers, and occasional disposals of capital items, old vehicles for example.

- Flows out: purchases, overheads, wages, loan repayments, payments of dividends to shareholders, your drawings (that is, your personal income) with occasional payments of taxes. Depreciation is ignored, as no cash moves.

- Timings: when the sales and purchase invoices are settled, not when they go out or arrive.

Why cash-flow forecasting matters

A simple, practical example is of Tom, a busy teacher with great woodworking skills, who makes mahogany boxes which are highly prized as Christmas gifts. It is now November and he is hoping to make around £3500 to buy his daughter an old car for Christmas.

Last month, October, he paid cash for £400-worth of timber, screws and other materials. Half of the boxes will sell for cash to colleagues from school (10 in November and 90 in December), and a local gift shop will take the rest this month but pay in February. He expects to make 200, and to sell them at £20 each. Fortunately his accountant sister-in-law calls in, and quickly sorts out a profit-and-loss budget and a cash-flow forecast.

What Tables 3.4 and 3.5 show is that Tom's profit does turn into cash eventually, but only in February. The bottom line of the cash-flow table gives the position month by month. To his dismay, he won't have got enough cash to buy the car before Christmas.

For anyone operating on a larger scale the warning is clear: forecast only your profit and you can easily run out of cash. Forecast your cash as well as your profit and you should survive (Table 3.6). Appendix 1 shows how to create a cash-flow forecast.

Table 3.4   Tom's profit-and-loss budget

Profit-and-loss budget to end December	
Invoiced sales: 200 × £20	£4,000
Materials	£400
Value added	£3,600
Overheads: trivial	—
Net profit	£3,600

Table 3.5   Tom's cash-flow forecast

Cash-flow forecast: October–February (£)					
	Oct	Nov	Dec	Jan	Feb
Income					
From cash sales	–	200	1,800	–	–
From sales to shop	–	–	–	–	2,000
Total income	–	200	1,800		2,000
Outgoings					
Materials	400	–	–	–	–
Cash flow for month	(400)	200	1,800	–	2,000
Cumulative	(400)	(200)	1,600	1,600	3,600

NOTE Brackets signify minus quantities.

Table 3.6   What to include in profit-and-loss budgets and cash-flow forecasts

	Profit and loss budget	Cash flow forecast
Sales invoices	all issued, whether or not paid	only shown when payment expected
Materials	the value used to make the goods sold	shows value when payment due
Capital equipment	not shown	shown when paid for
Overheads	the share for the period, whether or not invoiced or paid	shown when payment expected to be made
Depreciation	the share for the period	not shown – no cash moves
VAT	ignore it if you are VAT-registered	show it

Planning for profits

In planning for profits, the main tool is the profit-and-loss budget. In principle it is extremely simple (the numbers shown in Table 3.7 are just to show how it works).

Profit-and-loss accounting (known as P&L) answers the vital question: 'How much do I sell, what are my costs and so how much money do I make?'

Table 3.7   Profit and loss budget (£'ooos)

Sales invoiced			100
	Cost of sales (ie cost of the items invoiced)	40 – *Just labour plus materials*	
Gross margin			60
Overheads	Staff	9	
	Premises	5	
	Transport	3	
	Insurance	1	
	Depreciation	1	
	Other overheads	1	20 –
Operating profit			40
	Finance costs	1	
	Tax	2	
			3 –
Net profit			37

NOTE: If it is hard to say how much labour goes into each item sold, it is difficult to specify the cost of sales. The easy solution is to put labour into the overheads, leaving only materials in the second line down and substituting for gross margin the term 'value added'. That simply means the amount of value added to materials by your efforts. This is quite acceptable.

Accounting terms

A **budget** is a forecast that you are working to. When (NB, *not* if) events overtake it and it becomes out of date, you re-budget.

Control is the process of recording alongside the budget what actually happened, to alert you to dangerous deviations.

An **account** is a record of what actually happened over a period of time.

So you start off with predictions in a budget, or a series of budgets, then you report what really happened in an account. These terms can be applied to P&L, cash flow, capital expenditure, sales, staff costs or any other financial matter you want to keep track of.

By now you may feel the need for a summary of what the three main accounting documents do (Table 3.8).

Control of credit is another important matter. Selling goods on credit is, in effect, giving out something valuable to a stranger in return for a promise to pay. Put like that, it sounds as dangerous as it is.

In descending order of desirability, the best approaches to credit are:

(a) Get paid in advance.

(b) Get part-payment in advance.

(c) Get paid on delivery.

(d) Get paid as soon as possible after delivery.

(e) Don't get paid at all.

You will probably direct most of your efforts towards eliminating (e) and shortening the time under (d). A further penalty of giving credit is the admin load of keeping on top of who owes you what.

This whole topic of credit control is so important that we look more closely at it in the next section.

Table 3.8   Differences between profit-and-loss accounts, balance sheets and cash-flow forecasts

Profit-and-loss account	Balance sheet	Cash-flow forecast
Sales invoiced in the period, whether or not the customer has paid.	**How much** money is tied up in the firm. **Where** it is tied up.	**Income** – shows how much, and when, cash is expected to arrive.
Expenses incurred in the period, irrespective of whether the bill has been paid.	**What** were the sources of that money.	**Expenses** – shows how much cash is expected to be paid out, and when.
Depreciation is shown.	**Depreciation** is shown.	**Ignores** anything that is not an actual movement of cash – like depreciation.
REFERS TO A PAST PERIOD	REFERS TO A MOMENT IN TIME	REFERS TO A PERIOD IN THE FUTURE

Credit control

Once you start to give credit it is difficult to withdraw, so it is worth seeing if you can develop a strategy for avoidance.

When dealing direct with the public things are simplest. People expect to pay on delivery, even to place a deposit with order. In B2B, the assumption is that credit must be offered. Is that true? Probably not if your business has any of these characteristics:

- Small outlay. Nobody really minds paying the window-cleaner £20 from the petty cash.

- Emergency. If the only way the big problem can be solved quickly is to pay cash.

- Scarcity. The only person providing something that everyone needs can demand and get cash payment.

- Uniqueness. If the complete package that you offer really has outstandingly attractive features, people might swap their desire for credit for their desire for those features.

Credit cards remove bad debt if you follow their rules. As well as the public, many firms use them for small purchases. They cost you up to about 5 per cent of the sale value.

When dealing with firms you can argue that if they pay cash they save your costs, which you pass on to them. Don't be tempted instead to make a charge for credit or you may fall under the rules governing banking, a grim prospect.

Positive strategies for credit control

If you conclude that you have to give credit, these are the things to do:

- When selling, be suspicious if the order comes too easily – maybe they cannot get credit elsewhere.
- Carry out credit checks and before processing the order ask your customer about any court orders that are disclosed.
- For private limited companies, check on them and their directors via **www.gov.uk/government/organisations/companies-house**.
- When negotiating an order, make the payment terms an integral part of the deal.
- When dealing with anyone but the owner, and especially if it is a big firm, ask what the accounts settlement policy is: you may find that they always take three months' credit (many do).
- Depending on what they say and on your attitudes, either stand your ground and risk losing the order or modify the terms, including price, accordingly.
- Always know exactly who your firm is dealing with (see below).
- Get a specific undertaking about when you will be paid (eg seven days after delivery) and include it in your written confirmation of the order.

- Get a signature on a delivery note plus, if relevant, a satisfaction note.

- Invoice immediately on delivery.

Knowing who is placing the order may become very important, especially if disputes arise later. Create a simple form that you keep with order forms, and once the order is in the bag, say that you need one or two details to open the account. The form requires you to ask:

- the exact name, in full, of the organization placing the order;

- the customer's constitution – sole trader, partnership, limited company, charity, company limited by guarantee, public body, etc;

- names and addresses of sole trader or partners;

- names of directors, authorized and issued capital, registered office, country of registration and registered number of limited company (some of this you may be able to get from Companies House and some should be on their letterhead, which you may already have);

- two trade referees;

- bank name and branch address.

It is perfectly normal for a buyer opening a credit account to be asked for this information. To simplify the task, and to make it look routine, create a simple form that captures the information.

Another precaution may be to divide a large order into a number of deliveries, with agreement that you will be paid after each one. Provided you have something to that effect in your Terms and Conditions of Sale, you will be within your rights to hold back the next delivery until the last one has been paid for.

Should the boot eventually be on the other foot and you are asked to provide a reference for one of your customers, be careful. If you give unjustified positive information you can be sued for any damages that may arise. If you are unjustly negative, a suit for slander (if spoken) or libel (if written) may arise.

When you invoice, be sure that your invoices carry the following information:

- the information required by law (see Chapter 5, Your business name and legal status, for disclosure requirements);
- the charge and how it is arrived at;
- the date of issue, which is also the tax point for VAT-registered traders;
- any information that the customer requires, such as an order number or stock number;
- payment terms, shown prominently.

Statements are required by some customers. They are summaries of the transactions with the customer over an appropriate period of time, say three to six months. They are usually sent monthly, and show:

- all invoices issued during the period that the statement covers, those due (or overdue) for payment being marked accordingly;
- payments received during the period;
- the outstanding balance on the account.

(See Figure 3.1 for an example invoice and statement).

In view of the rising costs of administration and postage, many businesses now send statements only to those customers who insist on them. They can be a help to the customer in checking that their idea of what they owe you coincides with yours, and that you have registered the payments that they have made. The statements can also help you, by drawing to their attention overdue invoices. But you can chase overdue invoices just as effectively without issuing statements, so that alone is not sufficient reason for instituting them.

Figure 3.1 Example of invoice and statement

This is an *invoice*. It is simply a bill for goods supplied or services rendered.

	ABCD Ltd		
			700 High Street Anytown AN1 1AN
	Invoice		
Smith & Co 698 Cook St Anytown	*No:* 217/11 *Date and* *Tax Point:* 11/3/17 *Your Order:* 92/2709/pr		

Quantity	Description	Each	Value
8 cases × 24	Widgets no. 2050 ½"	£12.50	£100.00
	Goods		£100.00
	VAT @ 20%		£20.00
	Total payable		£120.00

PAYMENT DUE 30 DAYS FROM INVOICE DATE
Registered in England no 123456
VAT no 111.2222.33
Directors: A Allen, B Brooks, C Cliff, D Davis

	ABCD Ltd			
		700 High Street Anytown AN1 1AN		
To Smith & Co 698 Cook St Anytown		*Date:* 31/3/11		

Date	Invoice	Value	Payment	Balance
Brought forward				180.00
18/1/17	103	55.00		235.00
27/1/17	118	123.00		358.00
3/2/17	124	81.00*		439.00
5/2/17			180.00	259.00
28/2/17	183	97.00*		356.00
7/3/17			55.00	301.00
11/3/17	217	120.00		421.00
26/3/17			123.00	298.00
Balance carried forward				298.00

ITEMS MARKED* ARE OVERDUE – PLEASE PAY NOW
Registered in England no 123456
Directors: A Allen, B Brooks, C Cliff, D Davies

This is a *statement*. It summarizes the activity on this customer's account. The invoice shown above (no 217 for £120.00) is the last one on it. The information it gives is taken from the firm's books, and enables the customer to see if his books agree with yours. Most people get something similar every month – a bank statement.

When credit control fails

Whatever they may have promised, some customers will not pay on time. This affects your cash flow and so threatens your survival. Thus immediate, robust and effective action is called for:

- Keep a daily check on outstanding accounts.

- When an invoice falls due for which payment has not arrived, telephone to see if there is a problem. If there is one, sort it out. If none, extract a promise that the cheque will either go off that day or will be available for collection when you visit tomorrow by appointment as an agreed time.

- Explain that no more deliveries will be made until outstanding accounts are settled.

- Write, text or e-mail to confirm.

- Know your right to claim interest at Bank Rate (strictly speaking, the Bank's 'reference rate') plus 8 per cent, and fees, for late payment from business customers (see **www.payontime.co.uk**), but never claim interest from the public unless you are registered under the Consumer Credit Act.

Usually a firm but friendly approach will ensure that you get paid this time, and that in future they might smarten up, knowing that you mean business. It is not easy to swap roles from the salesperson to the account collector, but your survival depends on it. Put yourself in the other person's shoes for a moment: they know they have done wrong and they know you are in the right. This gives you moral authority.

A hardened few will still not pay. Try a final visit, armed with a copy of the invoice and delivery note to neutralize stories that they have got lost. Explain that you sold to them in good faith, they promised to pay but have not done so and that it is causing you cash-flow problems and difficulties with the bank. Ask for the money, there and then. There may be heated words. Ignore them. You have a right to be paid. If payment is not forthcoming, explain that you will need to sue for the debt. That should produce results, for once you start the court process the costs climb sharply and a losing defendant usually has to pay them.

If you can show written orders, conditions of sale and your confirmation of order, plus a signed delivery and/or satisfaction note, a County Court case should be straightforward. The Small Claims procedure is simple and applies to claims of up to £10,000 (£3,000 in Wales and Northern Ireland).

This can be done online through **www.gov.uk**. It takes about 30 minutes and fees are slightly lower than for the paper route. Alternatively you might prefer to use Mediation, a simplified service that costs £50 or £100 plus VAT for claims of up to £5000, but can deal with claims up to £50,000, compared with the Small Claims Court, which takes claims of up to £200,000.

Be aware that a judgment does not always mean you get paid, but it is the first step. Despite that, always pursue rogues via the law, not by way of threats, or the tables will turn on you.

Should you receive a solicitor's letter from the defendant, ignore any bluster and look only at the substance of the defence. If they have a serious case for not paying, or getting a reduction, try to settle out of court and, next time, don't let it get this far but make your case watertight from the start.

It may be worth trying a debt collector; perhaps you should meet one and see what they can offer, as part of your pre-start research. They might be cheaper and more effective than automatically steering everything towards a solicitor.

Breaking through to profitability

Once the P&L budget is complete, you are ready for the next stage of understanding how your firm works. The question we address here is this: 'How much do I have to sell before I make a clear profit?'

The answer lies in another simple piece of arithmetic, to calculate your break-even point. That is the level of sales which produces enough profit to meet all the costs. Once you have passed it, all the extra profit is yours... and the taxman's. Equally, if things go wrong, you will want to know the level that sales can fall to before you start to make losses. Table 3.9 makes the point (the budgeted numbers are, as always, just examples).

Divide the annual break-even sales figure into weekly numbers and make a note of them on your weekly and monthly sales budgets. That way you get early warning of profit trends, whether good or bad.

Table 3.9   Working out a break-even point

	Budget		Break-even (figures rounded)
	£		£
Sales	90,000		69,000
Materials	30,000	(33% of sales)	23,000
Value added	60,000	(67% of sales)	46,000
Overheads	46,000	(remains same)	46,000
Net profit	14,000		–

Calculating the break-even point

1 Budgeted value added ÷ budgeted sales = z per cent.

2 Overheads ÷ z × 100 = break-even sales.

3 Break-even value added = overheads.

4 Break-even materials = break-even sales *less* break-even value-added.

Alternatively, if you prefer charts to tables, you can adopt the break-even chart model shown in Figure 3.2.

One major benefit of using a chart is that it shows how important it is to keep costs variable, rather than fixing them. This is truest at times of greatest uncertainty, such as when the firm is new. Visualize pulling the fixed-cost line downwards and think how sharply the break-even point would move to the left, that is, to a lower level of sales.

Figure 3.2   Break-even chart

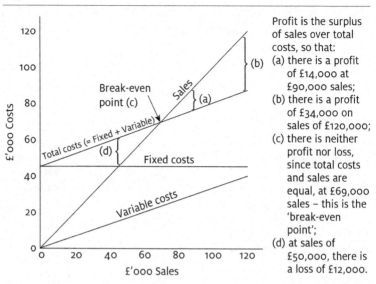

Profit is the surplus of sales over total costs, so that:
(a) there is a profit of £14,000 at £90,000 sales;
(b) there is a profit of £34,000 on sales of £120,000;
(c) there is neither profit nor loss, since total costs and sales are equal, at £69,000 sales – this is the 'break-even point';
(d) at sales of £50,000, there is a loss of £12,000.

Smarter costing

Once you are selling a range of products, simple absorption costing may no longer be adequate. You may wish to move to contribution costing. Once again, it is simple in concept, saying: 'We can't allocate every item of cost to each product; it's just too complicated. Instead we'll allocate just those things that clearly belong to each product. The rest we'll put into overheads, and they get paid from the general pool of profit.'

Table 3.10 shows how it works in a situation where a firm has three products with very different mixes of labour and materials selling at £30, £40 and £55.

Direct materials and labour are those used directly in the product, eg for a firm that presses DVDs, the disk, case, notes, outer box and labour for making and packing.

Indirect costs are those you are unable to allocate easily, such as rent, insurance, cleaning materials and machine maintenance, which go into overheads.

Table 3.10 Example showing contribution costing

Product:	X	Y	Z
Direct materials (£)	10.00	15.00	25.00
Direct labour (£)	2.00	18.00	5.00
Total direct costs (£)	12.00	33.00	30.00
Average sales value (£)	30.00	55.00	40.00
Contribution to overhead, and profit, per item (£)	18.00	22.00	10.00

One further calculation reveals the amount of money the firm plans to make. Taking the contribution that a single unit of the product yields (from the last line of table 3.10), then multiplying it by the number you plan to sell, reveals the total contribution to overheads and profit that you expect. This feeds straight into your P&L budget, providing its first two lines. Table 3.11 shows how.

Table 3.11 Example showing the total contribution

Product:	X	Y	Z	Total
Contribution to overheads and profit, per item (a) (£)	18.00	22.00	10.00	
Sales forecast (units) (b) (£)	2,000	3,000	500	
Total contribution (a) × (b) (£)	36,000	66,000	5,000	£107,000

Looking at the relatively small contribution that only 500 units of Z make, you might be tempted to discontinue it. That might be the right decision, but be aware that you will need to make up its £5,000 contribution from savings or price-rises elsewhere.

Doing this on a spreadsheet enables 'what-if' planning (What if I raise the price of Z by five per cent? What if I cut the price of X by £1? etc) to see what combination of pricing and volume produces the greatest total contribution.

CASE STUDY   The Irish take precautions

After 32 years managing projects in the construction industry Pat O'Brien suddenly found his job was redundant – not a comfortable situation for someone who had begun occasionally to think about what he might do in retirement. For some people a shock like that lays them out cold. For Pat, it acted like the most bracing cold shower imaginable.

The huge depression in building in Ireland at that time meant he could not conceive of finding another job in his specialist field. 'It certainly was a shock,' he says, 'But it was no good feeling sorry for myself – I had a living to earn. So I got a sheet of paper and wrote down all the things I was good at and all the things I liked doing. Health and Safety came singing out at me, so I looked around to see if I could possibly make a go of it.' That assessment was based on the H&S work that Pat had done in the past, but he wasn't sure if his qualifications were up to the mark so he planned to undertake further training. 'Although I knew I was pretty good at it, I did really need to broaden my scope. I knew from having had H&S responsibilities in a big firm how wide it ranged. That meant it was a headache for operating managers to keep on top of not only today's demands, but tomorrow's as well. There was my opportunity.'

From there it was just a short step to the vision behind Pat O'Brien Safety Ltd: a one-stop shop that met all of an organization's H&S needs for consultancy, training, services and products. 'I started with the customer's needs and worked out from there,' says Pat. 'Let's say a manager reads an inspector's report that says he or she needs, for example, better harnesses and some training for the staff using them. There simply isn't the time to go out shopping for products and trainers so the risk is that the recommendations aren't implemented, with all the risks that implies. Staff could be injured or worse, insurers may reject claims and the manager would get the sack. It was a problem crying out for a solution.'

Bearing in mind that Pat's experience was in a single industry, although an important one, he expected to have to learn a lot quickly. In that he was not disappointed. 'It's been a hair-raising ride,' he admits,

'But I'm amazed at how the business has taken off. It was a huge gamble to try to do everything in H&S from the word go, but it has really paid off. The whole business knits together into an integrated whole – an audit of a client's practices identifies problems; consultancy works out the best way to solve them; that often includes writing manuals, training and other services, which we provide; and there's the straight-forward sale of products needed to put the whole thing into practice. It makes sense for us and also for the customer.'

To keep the show on the road Pat O'Brien Safety Ltd employs four full-time staff and 50–100 freelance trainers and consultants. 'The free-lances are very important to us,' Pat says. 'They enable us to keep our fixed costs low whilst still being able to bid for contracts of any size. We have to have controls in place to ensure that they all work uniformly to our own high standards, but it has all worked well so far.'

And the future? Pat is aware of the limits imposed on the expansion of his business by geography. The population of the Irish Republic is under five million, and of Northern Ireland under two million. In total they are smaller than Switzerland (8.4 million). What other opportunities can he see beyond the point at which his H&S work might plateau?

One of the biggest challenges facing western societies is the rise in the number of dementia sufferers in the population. Ireland is no more exempt from this scourge than any other advanced country. People with the condition are, in many ways, unsafe physically, though that does not cover the full extent of their difficulties, which range across the spectrum of dexterity, cognition and vision. Whilst nursing homes and hospitals are already served by many suppliers with products that address these issues, Pat O'Brien has acquired the distributorship for the highly respected Memory Care range of aids. Supplies are only 70 miles away across the Irish Sea on the UK mainland and are backed up by highly professional designers and manufacturers. As Pat says: 'Our products won't cure dementia, sadly, but they can help to improve the lives of hundreds of thousands of my fellow Irish citizens.' He sets the goal of this arm of the business as 'simply to transform environments for a better life with dementia'. It would be hard to quarrel with that.

www.patobriensafety.com

Key jobs to do

- Decide on a costing system – relate this to pricing (Chapter 2).
- Calculate hourly charge rates for labour.
- Set up a system to monitor performance.
- Decide your policy on granting credit.
- Forecast your cash-flow situation.
- Prepare a P&L budget.
- Calculate your break-even point.

Raising the money

Grants: free money is best

There is not much free money around, but given that it is free, it is worth looking for. The website **www.gov.uk/business-finance-support-finder** offers a free search of its database ('online grants finder') for any money you might qualify for.

Generally speaking, money is available for projects that look likely to increase employment directly, or indirectly by developing a commercial proposition.

Here we discuss the situation in England; information on other parts of the United Kingdom is available from the websites of bodies listed above.

The Work Programme is a central government scheme designed to get long-term unemployed people into work. It offers employers grants of £50 a week or more, plus training grants. You have to pay the employee a conventional wage.

Regional Growth Fund and Selective Financial Assistance aim to encourage investment in deprived areas, including by new firms.

A government-backed company, **www.startuploans.co.uk**, can lend between £500 and £25,000 at six per cent interest over up to five years.

The Prince's Trust offers loans and grants to people aged up to 30 starting a business, plus the support of a volunteer mentor. I recommend them; I used to be one.

Other Schemes are featured on **www.gov.uk**.

Beg, steal or...

The principles behind bank borrowing are simple. For the lender, it offers a profit by hiring the money out for less than they have to pay to hire it in. Their back-up is that they will rarely lend unless they have some security or collateral, usually by taking a charge over some valuable asset. Then, if you don't pay, they sell your house and dip into the proceeds to clear the debt. If you do not have collateral, see the Enterprise Finance Guarantee scheme later in this section.

For the borrower, if it costs £10,000 a year to borrow £100,000 and he or she can make £30,000 by doing so, the motive is obvious.

Before assuming that borrowing is essential, see if you can devise a business model that avoids or minimizes it. Try seeing if you could:

- buy goods on credit, then take cash with order: you pay for purchases only after you have been paid;

- sell any personal asset (caravan? boat?) that you will have no time to use;

- release capital by moving to a cheaper house;

- stay put in the house but remortgage (housing loans are cheaper than business loans).

If none of those is possible or to your taste, the high street banks may be the next port of call. They offer three types of loan finance:

- overdrafts, suitable to cover the day-to-day fluctuations in your cash position;

- medium-term loans over up to five or seven years, for equipment;

- long-term loans from 7 to 20 years, for property purchases.

An important point is never to use overdrafts for longer-term finance. Overdrafts can be called in at a moment's notice, literally, and are quite unsuitable for anything but day-to-day needs.

Many other lenders exist, but extreme caution must be exercised. At least one of the usual banks can be expected to lend for any viable proposition. If they turn you down, look at yourself rather than blaming them, and avoid so-called secondary banks and money-lenders. As someone once said, if they are the answer it was a very silly question.

It ought not to be easy to borrow. Banks are putting shareholders' funds at risk when they lend and should conduct searching enquiries into the destination of their money. They should analyse and criticize your business plan, giving you a hard time.

That may seem perverse, but ask yourself this: who will put you in the best position, the lender who hands money out recklessly, knowing they can bankrupt you to get repaid, or the one who uses their experience to help you foresee pitfalls and develop your business plan, seeking to be repaid out of a healthy cash-flow?

It follows that your approach to the bank must be well-prepared and thought through. As they say, you get one chance to make a first impression.

Banks charge interest and fees, which they may present as inevitable but which can be negotiable. Ask about their fees as part of every discussion and ask for their reduction or removal. Try to get them to reduce the interest charged: even a quarter of one per cent is worth having.

Local bank officials are given lending limits above which they have to seek permission to lend. It is worth enquiring what your business manager's limit is, or their boss's limit. If the local limit is £100,000, you will not want to put in a proposal for a loan of £100,200, thus ensuring that the request has to go up the line to someone who has never met you.

The government offers the Enterprise Finance Guarantee scheme, aimed at removing the bar to growth that lack of collateral imposes on a small business. Its main features are:

- Seventy-five per cent of the loan is guaranteed.
- Borrower pays 2% extra interest on the outstanding balance.
- Loans up to a 10-year term and £1,000 to £1 million are covered.
- Borrowing firm must have a turnover of less than £41 million.
- Most of the main banks offer it.
- Most sectors and activities are eligible, but some are not.

The detail is on **www.gov.uk**.

In addition to the banks, finance houses offer loans to business. The basis is similar to the HP agreement the public is familiar with, but the term can extend up to 10 years. Security cover will be a primary concern. Alternatively, they offer long-term leasing arrangements.

Merchant banks are not interested in the minor league of business, but start-ups and young firms seeking from €1 million (around £900,000) of investment, some of which may be a loan, though most will be in shares. That is quite different from a loan, as the section on limited companies (in Chapter 5) will show.

Factoring may be of more use once your firm is established, but if you start off with blue-chip customers and substantial orders, factors could be interested immediately. A factor buys your debts from you for less than face value, then collects all of the money due from your customer. It is a useful way to minimize working capital requirements.

Making your case to private investors

Private investors, as compared to institutions like merchant banks, can be divided crudely into two distinct groups. On one hand there are those rich individuals who back new and young firms with an eye to making money by selling their shares some years later. On the other are crowdfunding investors, large numbers of people who individually invest small sums. Both are worth considering as a means of raising equity capital by selling shares in your firm. To do that, though, you will need to start off on some scale, or expect to get big fast.

Most people have seen *Dragons' Den*, the TV programme in which entrepreneurs pitch their business ideas to a panel of potential investors. Applicants have to present their case, backed up by whatever research they can supply to support their case. The 'dragons', experienced business people who are largely self-made and have money to invest in promising projects, question and challenge the proposers then decide whether or not to back the projects and haggle over what share their contribution will buy them. Not every pitch succeeds by any means, but a significant number do.

Whilst the programme's main aim is to entertain, it does give entrepreneurs at least a taste of how money is raised in this way. The so-called 'business angels' can be contacted through **www. ukbusinessangelsassociation.org.uk**, an organization of 18,000 members. Investors often want to be involved in the company's management which, if you pick the right one for you, can lend the new firm great strength. Picking the right personality is important, for the relationship will be close. Their involvement could prove intolerable in the hard times if you aren't entirely easy with one another when times are good.

Crowdfunding works quite differently. The entrepreneur puts up a proposal on the internet, seeking to raise a specified sum and offering a prospectus in return. People who choose to invest typically put in small sums – usually well under £100 – on the promise of high rates of return. Unsurprisingly, some sites offer introductions to equity investors. In 2012 14 crowdfunding companies formed the UK Crowdfunding Association. Its website explains the system: **www.ukcfa.org.uk**.

Under the Enterprise Allowance Scheme they can get tax relief on their investment. HM Revenue & Customs' website, **www.hmrc. gov.uk**, gives details.

Banks – all the same?

No they are not – it really is worth shopping around to decide where to do your business banking. Popping into branches on my local High Street revealed quite different offers. Taking the core offer as payments-processing and loans, they seek to differentiate themselves via the extras.

- The first offered free banking for 12 months and a refund of charges.

- The second gives 18 months of free banking, fixing its prices and with a choice of tariffs.

- The third again offers 18 months free, plus free electronic payments and a mobile app.

- Bank number four also gives 18 months free, seeks no arrangement fees (the sum the bank will charge for setting up a loan) and offers a free credit card for 12 months and a £500 overdraft facility.

Different business models will find that those offers appeal differently. The third, for example, will attract firms expecting large quantities of payments made electronically. To people dealing in cash, that aspect of the offer is meaningless.

Figure 4.1

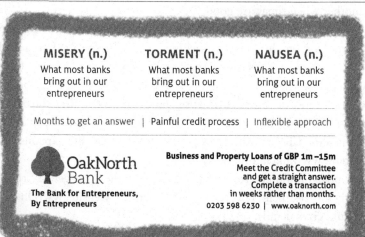

Many entrepreneurs find that their first choice of bank does not agree to fund them, or will do so but on disadvantageous terms. Consequently they may not be able to get the free extras that appeal most, but are forced to go elsewhere. No matter: the main thing is to fund the firm; relative to that the free extras are candy-floss. An ad from one of the challenger banks – banks set up within the last few years, rather than centuries ago – sums up many entrepreneurs' views of the High Street banks.

Presenting your case to the bank

An existing business seeking to borrow can present a record of achievement but even then has to persuade the bank to lend it the money. The new business finds the bar set higher and so must try harder.

Your presentation revolves around a written business plan. Do not worry about disclosing your secrets: bankers understand confidentiality. The plan should cover the following headings with no more than two pages, preferably less, on each:

- the service or product you plan to offer;
- markets, competitors, customers and why customers should buy from you;
- experience and background of key individuals, with personal bank details for the principals;
- premises and equipment, with costings;
- a monthly cash-flow forecast for year 1 together with a detailed P&L budget, plus outline plans for years 2 and 3;
- how much you want to borrow, what for, for how long and how you will repay;
- security, if any, that you can offer.

Do not doctor figures to make them look good but show what you can reasonably expect to achieve, for getting the money is only part of the job; once you have landed the loan you will be expected to fulfil your forecast.

Let the bank have all this a couple of days before the meeting. If you do not feel confident of doing it all yourself, get advice and help from either a business adviser or your accountant.

Finally, remember that some banks still think in terms of lending a pound for every pound you put in. This leads to the accusation that they are prepared to lend only to those who have. The banks reply that financial standing is not all; they are judging competence and character as well.

Cutting out the middleperson

Online peer-to-peer (P2P) lending is still seen by some as a fringe activity, yet it is growing rapidly. At the time of writing the medium is lending at the rate of over £1.8bn a year to SMEs. The government has put in £20m specifically to support SMEs. Some may see its rise as a response by savers to the minute interest-rates on offer from mainstream savings institutions: once interest rates rise, it is possible that they will flee back to the safety of building societies.

There is a useful summary of the field on www.moneysavingexpert. com/savings/peer-to-peer-lending#what.

Islamic banking

A core requirement of the Muslim religion is justice in all dealings. In business transactions, Islam sees the charging of interest as immoral since the lender has not invested labour in the enterprise. Interest-based lending shifts responsibility entirely on to the shoulders of the borrower, which is thought to be unjust. Instead, Islamic teaching requires lender and borrower to share the risk in a form of joint venture, with the reward to the lender as a pre-agreed share of any profits that might arise. These beliefs spring from the same religio-legal code (Shari'ah) that forbids gambling or pornography among other things judged capable of harming individuals and society. Prohibition of involvement in enterprises dealing in pork is a specific ruling that applies to Muslims and Jews alike.

Banks following Islamic practices need to make a profit just as do those following the western model. They do this in a number of ways that avoid the charging of interest, all of which are – as with any matter concerning religion – open to a range of interpretations. Fortunately there is now increasing consensus on the Shari'ah standards with which Islamic banks must comply.

Three financing models, broadly corresponding to the western approach, are popular among Islamic banks. None charges interest, all share profits (as well as the risk of losses) and all avoid prohibited enterprises. In certain cases, two or more of them can be combined:

- The bank buys the asset itself, then sells it on to the customer at a price that includes an agreed mark-up. The total amount is paid off in instalments. This differs from interest-based lending as the bank takes on risk by buying the asset in the first place.

- The bank buys the asset itself – which puts the bank at risk – and then leases it to the customer on an instalment plan. The method used to calculate the payments allows the bank its profit but does not involve interest. At the end of the lease the bank may choose to present the asset to the customer as a gift; it may not sell it to him or her, even for a trivial amount, as that would change the transaction from a lease to a sale.

- The 'common joint venture' model, of which there are two versions. The bank may advance all of the capital required, or the bank and the customer could join together to buy the asset, let us say a building or land. Two forms of repayment take place simultaneously: the borrower pays a rent to the bank for the bank's share, at the same time as buying-out that share by instalments. Once repayment is complete, the borrower becomes the owner of the asset. Over the term of the agreement, as payments are made, the bank's share of the asset falls, in what is termed a 'diminishing partnership'. This method can also be used for buying domestic dwellings.

As well as their lending, Islamic banks offer the full range of current account and credit card facilities expected from a bank.

CASE STUDY Clicktag

'It is amazing what you can accomplish if you do not care who gets the credit.'
Harry S Truman

'There is no limit to what a man can do so long as he does not care a straw who gets the credit for it.'
Charles Edward Montague

Somewhere in the afterlife the shades of those two giants, one an American statesman, the other an English journalist, may be slugging it out over who said it first. Meanwhile, in the 21st century, a woman-owned business, very much alive, is quietly getting on with the job. As far as its clients' customers are concerned, Clicktagmedia Inc of Ontario, Canada doesn't exist. But if they didn't, the clients would miss them and the customers might wonder what had changed. For Clicktagmedia's mission is to help their advertising-agency clients to shine at all aspects of marketing, but especially in the use of mobile media, without ever being visible themselves.

Melloney Campbell registered her digital design, marketing and development consultancy as long ago as 2009, but began operations in earnest only in 2015. They have so far established partnerships with firms in the US and several emerging technology providers around the world. She brings a wealth of experience to the task, gaining in-depth understanding of digital media over 16 years in that field, then serving as vice-president for communications for Canada's grass-roots self-help community, Startup Canada, a not-for-profit network of over 20 local groups of entrepreneurs who band together to help one another with advice and support.

What problem does Clicktagmedia solve for its clients? Melloney is clear: 'Ad agencies know very well what they are doing, across the entire field of their clients' communications and reputation. They know what their clients want, and what they need – not always the same thing. But it's not easy for them to stay up to date with developments in the fast-changing world of electronic marketing. Or they might, for one reason or another, have a problem with print, video or email marketing.' How does that work, specifically? 'Agencies have to look professional and at the top of their game in everything they do. When new media are called for – and these days that is more often than ever before – to do their best for the client they call us in. Digital isn't separate, it has to be woven in seamlessly with the rest of the communications activity, and we can help with any or all of its elements. We look at the issues, help to sort out the strategy if need be, and offer proposals.' But doesn't the client ask why they can't go direct to you for that part of their requirement? 'Absolutely not. We won't turn down a direct approach when it's made, of course, but where we are working with an agency we 'white label' the work; that is, we present it to the agency in a form whereby they can put their own name on it. Their client need never know. They're not cheating – agencies use outside suppliers all the time for all kinds of things and we're just the latest example of that established habit. The key thing always is the quality of the work, not who did it.' In any case, Melloney says, the agency's job is to look at the entire range of an advertiser's communication needs, whereas Clicktagmedia's is kept busy looking after its own specialist segments.

But surely, two people can't do all that unaided, however experienced, energetic and professional they are? 'Of course not. Just as the agencies call in outside help from time to time, so do we. There's a list of ten specialisms on our website that we can bring in at short notice, all of them stars in their field, to ensure the best possible outcome for our customer.'

Ms Campbell is emphatic about the reasons for Clicktagmedia's success: 'We are great at what we do, we have a proven track record of our creative resonating with the end audience and our work has garnered conversion rates beyond projected numbers. We are a silent partner to agencies, in other words – we make sure they look great!'

Asked what advice she would pass on to others thinking of following the path she has taken, Ms Campbell counsels research, research and research, as well as its close relative, due diligence (that is, careful, objective, in-depth investigation of all aspects of a proposed business arrangement). She also believes that it is vital to have an edge and to test this by asking yourself: 'Am I really solving a problem, or just reinventing the wheel? In the end, would I buy this proposition myself?' She also has a warning. Entrepreneurship is an all-or-nothing way of life, she believes, and advises that anyone unable to commit their life fully from the outset should consider starting off part-time. But she does not intend to discourage: 'If you're passionate, committed and have a solid support system such as a Startup Community, you're starting off right. Remember, you don't need to do it on your own.'

Despite her success, Melloney's ride hasn't all been smooth. Given the way that the Canadian business scene interacts with that of its neighbours to the south, she has found that many of her opportunities lie in the USA. 'In every sense, the USA is a different country and we didn't know about the government's programs to help us deal with foreign markets. We learned from experience what we could have found out about quite easily.' She also recognises now the existence of support systems to help women entrepreneurs which she wishes she had known of earlier. Also, she would have found greater financial literacy helpful.

So does that mean all the problems are solved? 'No way! Despite all the advances made, in our society businesswomen still do have a greater challenge with credibility; women in start-ups, even more so. There are jobs that we deserve to land which go to the more estab-lished, larger firms. That is really frustrating.' At some point in the future, Clicktagmedia will itself be seen as solid and established, but that day can't come fast enough for Melloney.

She issues a call to arms: 'What we need to do is set up a network of women entrepreneurs working together to create a large ecosystem that big brands could hire confidently,' she declares. It will be no surprise if she makes that happen, too.

www.clicktagmedia.com

Key jobs to do

- Investigate grants.
- Decide your financing strategy – how much do you put in, how much will you borrow and on what terms?
- Create and present your case to potential lenders.

Your business name and legal status

The options

Everything in this section refers to England and Wales, some to the UK as a whole. The lack of precision does not matter as, if you plan to adopt anything other than the simplest constitution for the business, you will need to take detailed advice from a lawyer, who will sort out any misunderstandings. What this section can do is enable you to form some views before consulting that august and expensive individual.

The main choices available are:

- sole trader;
- partnership;
- limited company;
- cooperative.

We shall address all of these except cooperatives. There are special organizations devoted to their development, and the best way into the system is Co-operative and Community Finance, **www. coopfinance.coop**. The situation described is true for England and Wales but there may be variations elsewhere.

Sole trader

By far the most popular way of getting into business, sole tradership is also the simplest. You simply notify HM Revenue & Customs so that they can change your income tax and NI status to self-employed. You will now pay NI contributions in Class 2 and Class 4.

Legally, you and the business are one. Anything the business does is your responsibility. If the firm fails owing money, **the debts are yours personally**.

It is wise to review all your insurances, particularly those for the house and car, to be sure that you are covered for using them for business. Cover for the car, especially, will almost certainly require changes.

Apart from following any regulations and acquiring licences that apply to the activity you plan to undertake, you are free to operate.

Partnership

In a partnership, two or more individual people are involved as principals of the firm. On the whole, partnership is much like sole tradership, with one important difference. In a partnership **each partner is personally responsible for** *all* **of the liabilities of the firm**. Common sense says it should be only for a share, but the law says otherwise.

It is clearly important to select partners with care; if one runs off with the money, those left behind are saddled with all of the debts.

Like a marriage, partnership can be subject to many strains, so just as celebrities arrange through a prenuptial agreement how their assets will be split on divorce, wise business partners have their solicitor draw up a partnership agreement before going into business together. If they do then fall out, at least the separation can be orderly.

Limited Liability Partnerships came to the uk in 2001 and offer limits to partners' responsibility for commercial debts – see the Companies House website. LLPs must be registered at Companies House.

Limited company

A limited company is very different from the other forms of constitution. Where partners and sole traders are legally inseparable from the business, a limited company is itself a separate 'person' in law. It has its own liabilities and obligations, quite apart from those of its owners, directors and employees.

The private limited company is the form most often used. If you wish to sell shares on the stock market and have a share capital of £50,000 you can become a public limited company (plc), but few starters do.

The company itself is responsible for its debts, not the owners or directors, the shareholders' responsibility being limited to the paid-up share capital. Since most small companies are authorized to issue £100 of shares, yet issue only two or three shares of £1 each, their paid-up capital is limited to that two or three pounds.

Because of this, institutions lending to limited companies almost always insist on a charge on the company's assets, which are usually worth a lot more than £3 (meaning they can send in the bailiffs if need be) and guarantees from substantial people, usually the owner-directors.

Shareholders own the company but need not be involved in running it.

Directors are appointed by shareholders and are responsible to the owners and the law for the way the company is run. They can also be employees of the firm and/or shareholders.

Although this situation has the potential for all kinds of arrangements between people, almost always the small limited company's shareholders are its directors, owning just one or two shares each.

Once the company expands and needs extra capital, it might attract an outside investor. If, for example, the investor requires a one-third share of the firm, more shares will be issued within the authorized limit of £100 to make that possible. The existing directors could issue to themselves a further two shares each, bringing the total between them to six, then issue another three shares to the investor. Nine shares would then have been issued, giving each of the three a third of the issued shares and hence a third of the company.

Under this arrangement the directors could issue the shares to themselves at face value, £1 each, whilst selling the investor's portion at the value of the investment made. If the firm has been going for some time, it may have made money that has been allocated to the directors as income, which they have not withdrawn but have left in the firm, appearing on the balance sheet as 'directors' loans'. Those loans will be converted into shareholdings, their shares being sold to them at a more realistic price than £1.

Although that is the situation in principle, in real life an investor would want more than three shares, so as to give flexibility if he wanted to sell on part of his holding to someone else. Owning three shares, he could sell only one-third, two-thirds or all of his holding; owning 300, he could sell much more finely tuned proportions. For that to be possible, the authorized capital would have to be increased and the other shareholders' holdings increased accordingly, but while the number of shares held by each shareholder would change from the simpler model, the proportion held by each of them would still be one-third. Each would still own one-third of the firm.

If the firm should go broke, the directors have no personal responsibility unless they have been negligent or are guilty of the offence of wrongful trading. The liquidator takes over, collecting the firm's debts and selling its assets. First to be paid are the government (wouldn't you know it), next employees, after them the secured creditors and finally the unsecured creditors, usually other businesses who have sold to the firm on credit. If anything is left it is split between shareholders, but usually there is nothing.

There is no obligation to record the existence of the business if you are a partner or sole trader, but a limited company must be registered at Companies House. A solicitor, chartered accountant or company formation agent will set one up from scratch for you, but a cheaper and therefore popular option is to buy a firm that has already been set up and is ready to trade. This costs under £300. A web search will reveal many company formation agents.

The accounts of limited companies must be audited profession-ally once they reach a certain size or under particular conditions. For most small firms auditing is not required. The main exceptions are once turnover reaches £6.5 million or assets £3.26 million, or if the firm is regulated by the Financial Conduct Authority (FCA).

The accounts, in the form of a balance sheet and other docu-ments, must be filed at Companies House by a certain deadline, with a fee, and also be sent to members (that is, shareholders). If the filing is undertaken online, no fee is taken – though some of the necessary documentation may be charged for.

Your business name

The choice of business name is primarily a marketing decision, but there are legal ramifications. Ideally, a business name is expressive, attractive, memorable and has a leading initial near the start of the alphabet so that it appears high in listings. As with all marketing activ-ity, look carefully at the name from the point of view of your customer. Ask other people for their opinion. A wise precaution is to use one of the online translation tools to check that the name chosen has no adverse meanings in all the markets you could conceivably sell in.

The rules governing the names that limited companies may use are operated by Companies House. Generally, they exclude names that:

- are criminal;
- are offensive;

- are already registered;
- suggest government approval;
- are misleading.

There is more to it, all explained on the Companies House website, **www.gov.uk/government/organisations/companies-house**.

Anyone, limited company, sole trader or partnership, may use a trading name other than their own. If they do so, their true name and address must be disclosed on all business documents for suppliers, employees and customers. In addition, a notice must be displayed 'prominently' in parts of business premises accessed by customers. The notice must take a specific form, as shown in Figure 5.1.

Finally, this information must be disclosed in writing immediately it is requested by anyone with whom anything is discussed or done in the course of business. It is important to comply or you could commit a criminal offence and moreover might not be able to make your contracts stick.

There are rules about what qualifies as someone's own name. Take someone whose given name is John Smith:

- John Smith;
- J Smith;
- Mr J Smith.

Figure 5.1   Notice to be displayed by businesses using a trading name

PARTICULARS OF OWNERSHIP OF
(*insert trading name*)
AS REQUIRED BY SECTION 29
OF THE COMPANIES ACT 1981

FULL NAMES OF PROPRIETORS:
(*insert names*)

ADDRESSES WITHIN GREAT BRITAIN AT WHICH DOCUMENTS CAN BE SERVED ON THE BUSINESS:

(*insert addresses*)

John goes into partnership with his mother, Jane. Their 'own names' are:

- J & J Smith;
- Jane and John Smith;
- John and Jane Smith;
- Smith's.

Mother pulls out and John forms a partnership with Tom Brown. Their own names are:

- T Brown and J Smith (and vice versa);
- Thomas Brown and John Smith (and vice versa);
- Messrs J Smith and T Brown (and vice versa).

In due course Jane Smith buys a limited company off the shelf, called Tetrablank Ltd. She trades in that name, the company's own name.

In all of the above examples, using any of these 'own names' means there is no separate business name to disclose.

However, any of these individuals or combinations of people might sense that marketing reasons dictate the use of a name that says what they do, rather than who they are. They might choose a name like John Smith Engineering Supplies or Victorian Woodworkers.

None of those names is the name of a person or company involved. They may use the names, but only if they disclose the ownership, as described earlier. In everyday dealings they will describe themselves as 'T Brown and J Smith trading as John Smith Engineering Supplies' or 'Tetrablank Ltd trading as Victorian Woodworkers'. 'Trading as' is often abbreviated to 't/a'.

In those last examples the letterhead would feature the trading name prominently across the top. The declaration of ownership will be in small, but clearly legible, print along the bottom, along with the other details such as VAT registration, registered office address for a limited company and so on.

CASE STUDY   Make your own cider, the hi-tech
Taiwanese way

In 2014 Alchema Inc won a competition for start-ups in its then home country of Taiwan. Its idea was for a revolutionary kitchen product: a device that would allow someone to make cider, mead or wine from fresh fruit in only two weeks. Co-founder and CEO Oscar Chang explains: 'Lots of people have tried home-brewing. Most have given up and many more would like to try but are put off by the complexity. Our secret lies in making everything simple for the customer. With the Alchema system, anyone can do it – all you need is a supply of fruit, water and a mains electricity connection. It's as easy as making coffee, but much more delicious. And it works every time.'

Anyone who has a few fruit trees knows that the harvest all comes at once. They try to give the surplus away to friends and neighbours, but most of them have the same problem. Turning the excess fruit into something good to drink that is also preserved by its own alcohol is an attractive idea. Of course, shop-bought fruit works just as well.

The Alchema system is more than a simple fermentation vessel, though. Many home-brew failures are caused by invisible impurities, so Alchema incorporates a medical grade UV-C LED light to sanitise the container before fermentation begins. Once it has started, for the traditional brewer there follows a period of uncertainty and waiting while mysterious processes take place, but the Alchema user can keep up to date with what's happening via a smartphone App until the exact moment when the batch is ready.

For centuries yeasts have been mankind's unwitting allies in its search for the benefits that alcohol can bestow; for decades electronics have helped the large-scale producers in their quest for perfection; now, in the 21st century, the Internet of Things is bringing understanding and simplicity to the human element of brewing in the domestic kitchen.

So, do Mr Chang and his 10-strong team which includes five co-founders, think that all the firm's problems are solved? 'Not at all. New problems keep on presenting themselves all the time, but we're up to the challenge. We've got the skills, we've got the motivation and we really believe in what we're doing,' he says. 'The nearest competitors – there are three of them – haven't got our technology. Ours is the only system that can sense what stage fermentation is at and talk to its user about it, and it's all protected by patents.'

Getting from the initial idea to a tangible, working product was a huge problem, even for an electrical engineering doctoral candidate. Until Alchema hit on the HAX Boost program in San Francisco, California, that is. In six weeks it moved the company into a position where it had manufacturing capacity and potential customers. HAX's support meant so much that the firm has now moved to California.

Alchema's chief challenges now are common to many SMEs making durable products. Once they've started up and proved their concept, to move to the next phase any company needs capital for tooling and creating stock, as well as to live off before the cash starts rolling in. 'It's a big dilemma, how to raise capital,' Mr Chang says, 'If we borrow it, the terms won't necessarily be favourable and the interest needs paying on time; if we sell equity, it can take ages to get the right investor, and even then they might demand a bigger share of the company than we feel is right.' He also believes that Angel investors are looking for companies where the costs fall proportionate to income, rather than ones like Alchema where he feels that they will be more or less in step. Nonetheless, a Kickstarter campaign in 2016 raised over $300,000 from 900 backers, each contributing an average of $38 against a request for $20 minimum (https://www.kickstarter.com/projects/alchema/alchema-turn-fruit-into-personalized-craft-cider).

Whilst he is proud of the team's achievements, Mr Chang does have some regrets, mostly about the impact of the business on his personal life. 'My family didn't understand – and how could they, I didn't quite realize it myself – how demanding the business would be. Whilst we obviously plan ahead, all sorts of unexpected emergencies arise that have to be dealt with and, as I'm CEO, the buck stops with me. Even when things are fairly quiet, there's a flood of emails and new customer enquiries demanding to be dealt with, all of which take time. Indeed, at the moment I have hardly any time to myself, but I'm sure it will all be worth it in the end.'

Mr Chang's advice to anyone in the position he was before 2014 is quite clear: nothing gets done without commitment to action. 'Clarity comes from engagement, not thoughts,' he says, 'You can't achieve anything just by thinking about it. So go ahead and get your hands dirty.'

And when you've done that, sit back, relax and enjoy a drink.

www.alchema.com

Key jobs to do

- Consider seeking advice on the best constitution for you.
- Understand the implications for costs, NI, taxation and raising money.
- Observe requirements for disclosure of ownership.

Business and the law

Employment law appears in Chapter 10, Employing people.

You should note that, whilst many countries' legal systems display many similarities, all jurisdictions have their own, unique aspects. This book deals with the law of England and Wales.

Civil and criminal law: how the difference affects you

The two systems of law have grown from completely different roots. Civil law came about from old statutes, interpreted by innumerable decisions by judges down the ages, resulting in a generally agreed set of rules for the way people should behave. An award in a civil case results in one party compensating the other. The burden of proof is a 'balance of probabilities'. The state is not interested in civil quarrels, so the police and the Crown Prosecution Service (CPS) stay away.

Criminal law is completely different. It arises from laws passed in Parliament and the sanctions are fines, imprisonment or community service. It is enforced by the police and the CPS, as well as many other public servants, including HM Coastguard, Trading Standards officers and others.

As is well known, the true penalty for losing a civil case may not be the court award but the legal costs, which for anything complicated quickly run up into the tens or hundreds of thousands of pounds.

There are two golden rules: for a civil case, keep the action short and settle well before it comes to court; for the criminal law, stay on the right side of it.

The civil law affects business owners mainly through two of its many branches: contract law and tort.

Contract law

The civil law of contract is extensive. Knowing some aspects of it helps the small business to form contracts that are valid and to recognize infringements of its rights.

In law, a contract is formed when three conditions are present:

- offer: an offer to buy, which may be subject to conditions;
- acceptance: an acceptance of the offer;
- consideration: some sort of exchange, in business usually money.

Thus if I offer to wash your car for a pound and you accept, we have a contract. I must do the work and you must pay me. But when must it be finished? To what standards of cleanliness? Who will supply the water, bucket and cloth? When will you pay me? Those questions illustrate why wise parties confirm contracts in writing. Except for land sales in England, Wales and Northern Ireland, an oral agreement is still a contract – it is just difficult to prove its exact nature unless it is written down.

If I had offered to do it for a bag of plums from your tree, or for you to babysit my children, it would still be a contract. If I said I would do it for nothing, no contract would exist as the third condition, 'consideration', would be absent.

In general, the best guide is to:

- tell the truth;
- keep your promises;
- know your obligations and keep to them;
- know and respect your customer's rights;
- never promise what you cannot or may not be able to deliver;
- always express clearly any doubts or uncertainties;
- be able to prove what you say is true;
- behave fairly and reasonably;
- make conditions clear;
- read and understand even apparently routine documents before signing;
- confirm your understanding of any agreement in writing;
- make proper use of professional and official advice.

When buying, check carefully that your understanding of the offer is the same as the seller's and get a written statement of exactly what the proposal is.

Most disputes arise not from deliberate misbehaviour but simple misunderstanding. So cut down the area open to misinterpretation and you reduce the risk of dispute.

Tort

Tort is defined as a civil wrong. The word is, appropriately, modern French for 'wrong' and came into English law via the Norman Conquest. The civil wrongs are, with a brief and inadequate explanation of each:

- nuisance: smells, noise, obstruction, etc;
- defamation: causing damage to reputations;
- conversion: selling stolen goods, even if acquired innocently;
- trespass: entering property uninvited;
- passing off: pretending that goods came from somewhere other than their true source;
- false imprisonment: unreasonably detaining someone;
- negligence: generally, carelessness or recklessness.

Of that list, negligence is the tort most likely to be committed by small firms. Having a loose stair carpet at the office is careless. To ignore someone's warning about it is reckless. If someone then trips, falls and suffers injury, they may sue you for negligence. In practice, you would hand the whole thing to your insurance company, but a shock may be in store if the policy requires you not to act negligently.

Not only might you have damages and legal costs to pay, but the Health and Safety Executive (HSE) might decide to prosecute you. Since the legislation they invoke is part of the criminal law, you might get a fine or prison sentence on top.

Going to law

Ideally, this is best avoided. If it cannot be avoided, keep your involvement short. In most cases small businesses have more to lose by loss of management time and concentration than by settling the case quickly. As a famous judge, commenting on the cost of lawsuits, once remarked: 'The law is open to anyone, just like the Ritz Hotel.'

There is one exception, where you are owed £10,000 or less under the jurisdiction of English law. The case will go to the County Court, but you may elect to have it dealt with by the Small Claims Procedure. This is a simple arbitration procedure designed for straightforward cases, conducted in private by the arbitrator with just yourself, the defendant and any witness or representative that may be needed. The procedure was designed to encourage DIY lawsuits, so you may not need a representative unless the case is at all complex. If you win, you will get back the court fees plus your costs in addition to any award. If you lose, you forfeit the fees and meet the other side's costs. A phone call to the local County Court will produce the forms.

The cost of solicitors deters people from using them, but there are occasions when they can actually save money by getting quickly to the nub of an issue. The worst way to use them is to try DIY, get into a tangle and then ask them to sort things out.

Contingency fees are a mixed blessing. This is the arrangement where a solicitor takes on a case, not for a fee but for a share of the award. It does ensure that poor people have access to the law, but no lawyer takes on a contingency fee case unless they are sure of victory. So the plaintiff could have won, paid a fee after the award and been better off. Fees might even have been awarded against the defendant.

If entanglement with the law is inevitable, ask around for a solicitor with a reputation for success in the kind of case concerned and pay whatever is necessary, giving clear instructions that you want the action concluded quickly and cheaply.

The risk of an adverse result is small, but if it happens to you the cost will be high. You may wish to consider legal expenses cover as part of the firm's insurance. It will not pay awards or fines, but it does meet the legal costs.

Contracts to buy

Pop into the newsagent's, put a coin on the counter and say 'Star, please'; when the newsagent hands it over the contract to purchase is complete. Leaving aside your poor taste in newspapers (in my opinion), as you collect your change you can reflect that most contracts to purchase are formed just as unthinkingly as the one you lately concluded.

When buying for business you need to adopt a more rigorous approach. Examination of the signature box on an order form will disclose that a signature means you accept their terms and conditions of sale, which no member of staff is authorized to vary. These terms may be on the back of the form, in a tiny typeface, in a tasteful shade of light grey. Few people except their creator have ever read them. Yet the point of them is to absolve the seller of responsibility for pretty well anything.

In 1977 the Unfair Contract Terms Act came into law to limit the exclusions allowed. Specifically, excluding liability for death was disallowed. Excluding liability for losses due to negligence, or for poor-quality and defective goods, is permissible only if reasonable. 'Reasonable' is a wonderful word that crops up all over the place in law. The courts usually judge it on:

- what information was available to each side before the deal;
- whether it was a standard-form purchase or the deal was negotiated;
- whether the purchaser had the power to get better terms.

Essential checks to perform are that the written contract gives accurate:

- prices;
- quantities;
- delivery dates;
- payment terms.

During the negotiation phase you may be able to improve your position by asking for:

- unfavourable terms to be deleted from the standard conditions;
- deletion of the seller's protection from the consequences of negligence or the supply of defective equipment;
- better terms than are on offer as standard, such as free training or after-sales support.

Do not just ask but treat it like a sales task. You have to show why the offending condition is wrong for you and for your relationship with the seller.

Your major purchases are likely to be gone over carefully. It is in the routine activities, the business equivalent of popping into the newsagent's, where the main risks lie. See the case study in the box.

Purchasing case study

- You need 200 three-foot lengths of timber. The product is sold in two-metre lengths.

- You allow for five per cent wastage and calculate that you will still get two three-footers out of a length, so you order 100 of the two-metre lengths.

- When the load arrives a lot of the lengths are under 2m, too short once your wastage is taken into account.

- You phone to complain and they tell you there is a condition on the back of the order you signed, which also appears in the back of their brochure, to say they can vary length by up to 10 per cent. That 10 per cent plus your 5 per cent makes the offending pieces under-length for your purposes.

- You conclude there is nothing to be done. You deliver late and too few to your customer and have the substandard lengths cluttering your store for the foreseeable future.

- You resolve to specify more carefully next time.

When the purchases arrive, do not accept them if unacceptably damaged. If the carton is broken and there might have been theft, either refuse the delivery or sign for it 'damaged and unexamined'.

Always examine deliveries on the day of arrival. There will be rules in the small print about how soon after delivery complaints will be entertained, and the seller will retain paperwork only in line with that timetable. If there is a complaint, make it immediately and always confirm in writing the same day, keeping a copy.

Contracts to sell

Here the tables are turned; you are now the one seeking maximum advantage, or a least not to be disadvantaged.

My view is that while terms and conditions of sale are necessary for your legal protection, they can also serve a marketing function by communicating your reasonable expectations and requirements of your customer. That means writing in clear language and legible type.

Seeing it as a marketing issue, I believe that firms should construct their own, handing them over to the solicitor to make completely sure they are legally effective.

Because this can be a daunting prospect, a prototype is offered of a set of terms and conditions of sale (see Appendix 2). Its purpose is to provide a draft that you can customise to your personal circumstances. Hack it about freely: that is what it is for. But do get your solicitor to check the result.

Conditions, warranties, guarantees and exemptions

Any contract, whether buying or selling, incorporates conditions and warranties. Conditions are really important matters, the breach of which entitles the other party to its money back plus damages. There are also implied conditions which need not be spelled out but are automatically present in all contracts:

- Seller has the right to sell – eg goods not stolen or on HP.

- Goods comply with the description – eg if reconditioned, not sold as new.

- Sample corresponds with bulk: the example you have been shown is truly representative.

- Goods are of suitable quality and fit for use.

The final item needs expansion. 'Suitable' quality is that which is 'fit' for the use to which the customer can be expected to put the purchase.

Exceptions are allowed, where the seller points out a fault or the buyer gives the article the sort of inspection that might reasonably be expected to reveal the fault.

Warranties are less important, entitling the injured party to damages only. They include many of the topics covered in the draft terms and conditions in the appendix referred to above.

Guarantees may be given with items you buy-in as components. That is helpful, but does not deflect your liability for what you sell. The customer's redress is to the person who supplied them, namely you so you have to put things right at your expense and then chase your supplier for satisfaction. If you issue guarantees, be sure that they say that they do not affect customers' statutory rights. Remember, too, that whatever the written guarantee may say, in law there is no time limit to the customer's rights, only what is 'reasonable' in the circumstances.

Exemptions can be criminal offences, where the trade or public are deprived of their legal rights – hence the disappearance from the shops of signs such as 'No refunds on sale goods'. The law is more relaxed about hired goods and sales to business customers, where there may be 'reasonable' exclusion clauses. If it affects you, take legal advice for it is a complex field.

Product liability

Until recently the United Kingdom did not have the level of product liability that exists in the United States, but we are moving rapidly in their direction. A supplier's responsibilities include efforts to:

- warn about potential risks – 'may contain nuts';
- inform consumers about risks and precautions – 'once cooked, it will be hot: handle with care';
- monitor product safety by recording and investigating complaints;
- test products;
- act if a problem is found;
- not to sell something you know, or ought to know, is unsafe;
- notify the authorities of unsafe products.

There are obviously special risks in certain categories: food and drink, toys, medicines and mechanical or electrical items come tomind. Specific regulations apply to many such categories: the government website gives information, **www.gov.uk/guidance-product-liability-and-safety-law**. In general, Trading Standards Officers, basedat county, unitary and city councils, are willing to give advice on how to avoid breaking the law in this and other ways, including the labelling of packaging.

At the back of all this is the threat that the authorities may take enforcement action if you do not comply, resulting in fines or imprisonment, and that injured parties – not just direct customers – could sue. Once again, insurance cover is advised.

Copyright, registered designs, trademarks and patents

Under these headings the law gives varying degrees of protection to intellectual property.

Copyright is the weakest. It gives automatic protection to anything original on paper – text, music, names, drawings, etc. A copyist need not change much to claim that his is also an original work. To make potential copyists aware that you know your rights, insert a ©, your name and the date at the start. If it could be important later to prove the date, send a copy to yourself through the post, conspicuously and securely sealed; check that the postmark is legible and keep it unopened in a safe place.

Copyright in artistic products lasts for the life of the author plus 70 years.

A trademark can be registered at the government's Intellectual Property Office (**www.ipo.gov.uk**) and you can search their database to ensure that yours really is novel. Trademark agents will do this for you if you prefer. In case your first preference has been taken, think up a stock of five or six names you would be happy to use and work through until you find a vacant one.

Registering your own mark gives unequivocal protection to you as its owner, or it should. Unfortunately it is not foolproof as there is no requirement for a mark to be registered, so you could unwittingly use one not registered, but in widespread use for decades and therefore entitled to protection.

Registered designs give better protection than copyright. For both trademarks and registered designs the services of an agent are necessary. Protection is for 25 years from registration, provided it is renewed every five years. Whilst the government's online registration fee is only between £50 and £150, professional advice can easily raise the total cost to £500 to £2,000 or more.

Patents give the highest level of protection. When applying it is vital to be able to declare that you have never 'disclosed' the item, that is, told anyone about it except for a patent professional. A full patent gives 20 years' protection from the date of filing the first application.

An agent will probably advise an initial application, cheaper and simpler than a full application, to establish your place at the head of any queue and give you a year in which to test the market, study feasibility, work out manufacturing methods or even find a buyer and decide whether or not to proceed. You will need a patent agent and deep pockets, as the cost of an initial application could be £5,000 over up to five years.

As with any other protection scheme, the real test comes when you have to repel a copyist. Patent lawyers are even more expensive than their common or garden counterparts, so it is wise to insure your registrations.

CASE STUDY Borrow not for long for a song through Gaifong in Hong Kong

Hong Kong is known worldwide as probably the most entrepreneurial city on earth. Visitors find it stimulating and tiring in equal degrees – the sheer energy of the place and its people is exciting at first but after a while it causes the visitor to develop a strong need for a comfortable couch in a silent, darkened room. Yet, even as the jaded visitor rests, the Hong Kong people toil away tirelessly.

Elliot Leung is typically imaginative. His neighbours all need the same household goods as anyone in any other advanced economy, yet living accommodation in Hong Kong is scarce and dwellings are therefore not large. The problem of storage is considerable. Why not, he thought, find a way of opening up everyone's possessions for hire to neighbours? That way nobody would need to own every appliance they ever needed to use, but could borrow whatever they needed and return it as soon as its usefulness was over.

(His idea caused me to look at my own garage – seven bicycles, many hand tools, an electric paint-stripper, a powerful sander for floors, a lawn-mower, a leaf-blower, ladders, battery-chargers, a heavy roller, tents and many more things besides, few of them used for more than a few hours per year. And that's just the garage.)

'The problem is really quite obvious,' says Elliot, 'But the solution wasn't easy to see at first. If somebody was willing to lend, let's say a Play Station for a weekend, how would they know they would ever get it back? How did they know that the person borrowing it was who they said they were? Would people want a hire fee? If so, what legal situations could arise if something got broken or a person was hurt? The more I thought about it, the more of a nightmare it became.'

Elliot was able to iron out all those problems and many more before launching his company in 2014. As founder and CEO of Gaifong ('neigh-bours' in Cantonese), he is unashamed of his background. 'Geeks, nerds and idealists, that's what we are, and we have social as well as business goals. We believe that sharing resources brings people together; that forms sounder neighbourhoods which in turn lead to a stronger society. If we can make a living at that, everybody wins.' It works – sometimes Gaifong's network leads to people borrowing from near-neighbours in the same apartment block. Not only does that help people to meet people, it means that delivery can be almost instantane-ous. 'There's also an environmental argument: more sharing means fewer things needing to be made and thus greater kindness to the planet,' he adds.

So far Gaifong employs six and Elliot has strong views on hiring staff. 'Hire only the top 1 per cent of talent – it's the only thing that matters in the medium to long term,' he claims.

Gaifong's system works through a smartphone app. After a free download, the user lists any unused or lightly used items that they would be willing to hire out. A borrower can browse all the offers in the category sought and see their location, picking the one that's most convenient. Bookings and payment operate through the system, though credit-card transactions are handled seamlessly by an independent secure contractor. When an item is booked, the system takes a security deposit, which is returned once the item is returned in good condition. Owners get regular payments and borrowers and owners can review and rate one another.

'When we had the idea we could see that it was a chicken-and-egg one,' says Elliot, 'Either we could look for lots of people with items to rent out who were waiting for a hirer, or we could try to recruit borrowers and then find items to rent to them. We went for the first option – with the benefit of our experience, it's the one I'd always recommend. Along with making sure that the customers, on both sides of the deal, find us and each other reliable. That is critically important.'

Recognition from Hong Kong's business community has been rapid. Gaifong and Elliot have been awarded Top 20 Startups in Hong Kong by *Hong Kong Business* Magazine and the Roadshow EcoStar Award. The company is also one of the small number accepted on to the HK Cyberport Incubation program and has been helped by the HK Cyberport Creative Micro Fund (CCMF).

And the future? Gaifong is aware that the space problem in Hong Kong is especially acute, but it is not the only city whose residents would like to release more living-space in their homes. On the website it asks people to name their city; once they have 10 from the same place, they will open the service there. So the potential is limited only by the number of cities on the planet – quite a market to go at.

Video interview: http://video.cnbc.com/gallery/?video=3000557360
www.gaifongapp.com

Key jobs to do

- Identify and understand the ways in which criminal law and official regulations affect your business.
- Understand how the civil law affects your business.
- Create terms and conditions of sale and have a solicitor approve them. Incorporate them in your sales stationery.
- Put up appropriate notices.
- Review your need for protection of intellectual property.

Premises

Can you work from home?

Many firms start this way and some never leave. Few neighbours would like their residential area turned into an industrial estate, so the main issues in British planning law are:

- the amount of noise, smells and other nuisance generated;
- the number and type of visitors;
- the visible evidence of business activity;
- quantity and type of traffic created.

The ultimate sanction is a letter from the local authority inviting you to cease operations or apply for planning consent (which will almost certainly be withheld). Failure to comply will lead to court action and hefty fines.

In addition, your family may have views about losing a bedroom, garage or study. The house may be subject to covenants that prohibit business activity, but it is difficult for even neighbours to have them enforced. (Covenants are in the title deeds for the property.)

On the other hand, many small firms operate from home in complete harmony with neighbours, sometimes so unobtrusively that people do not realize what is going on. Therein lies the answer: the operation needs to be so low key as to be virtually invisible and inaudible, creating no nuisance and run with total consideration for the interests of neighbours. See **www.planningportal. co.uk/info/200130/common-projects/56/working-from-home**.

To be blunt, the vast majority of those home-based firms that are closed down by officialdom deserve all they get. Work in progress parked on the verge, old engines in the front garden, the smell of paint and the noise of hammering: nobody should have to live next to it. Contrast that behaviour with my neighbour's. Everyone knows he runs his business from the garage, and those of us who are customers have been inside it. Occasionally a big lorry delivers materials, but it presents no problems. His customers are fewer than a dozen a week and all arrive by car, a level of activity exceeded by private individuals with a busy social life. It is difficult to imagine why anyone should complain.

Working from home does present a temptation that should be resisted, to do costings that assume accommodation is free. Better to price in what commercial premises would cost so that when expansion or some other force pushes you out into the commerical property market your prices do not suddenly jump. Other people manage to pay proper rent, so why not at least pretend you do?

Insurance is a big issue. Running your business will automatically void your domestic cover, so disclose your plans to your insurers and get things straight. It will cost more, but still be far cheaper than having a major claim refused.

If you have a mortgage, the lender has a right to know. This ought to be no more than a formality.

If your property is rented, the landlord needs to know your plans so as to notify his or her insurers. You may be asked to pay any extra premium.

Finding small premises

The premises now being provided for new businesses are a far cry from the retired chicken sheds in which earlier generations of entrepreneurs began work – miserable places with the huge benefit that they cost almost nothing. Newer premises are built to modern standards of heating, insulation and finish, take health and safety into account and consequently are not cheap.

In country areas there may be the chance to rent a disused building from a farmer or landowner. The system requires you to get planning consent and to convert it to modern standards. Many new firms overlook this point, running in the way their forefathers did, on the lowest overheads possible and with no security of tenure. This last point may not matter unless you need to borrow: lenders want to know if you have the right to operate from your premises at least until their loan is paid off.

If you should go along the conversion route, allow for the costly extras of mains water, drains, lavatories, electricity, gas if available, security, disability access, vehicle parking spaces and turning areas, plus possibly acceleration/deceleration lanes into the entrance, depending on the character of the road outside. The authorities will insist that everything is done to the highest standards. Once you are in the official system there are no short cuts.

Planning permission

Using any land for industrial or commercial purposes requires planning consent. Former occupants may have got away with not applying, but you may not be so lucky. Where you are renting or buying formally, this is unlikely to be an issue, but the informal market is different.

If you can trace back continuous usage for ten years (less in some cases), you may apply to the planning authority for a Lawful Development Certificate, a document that says, in effect, that you have consent to continue something that has gone on for so long that it is part of the scenery. The only problem with this is that it will tie you down very tightly to specific activities, constraining your flexibility in the future. On **www.planningportal.co.uk** search 'lawful development certificate'.

If you want to move from the existing planning consent, the government-imposed fee will be at least several hundred pounds, with no guarantee of success. There is a fee calculator at **www.planningportal.uk**. If the planning officer seems helpful you might feel confident enough to DIY, but otherwise a planning specialist (architect, town planner, surveyor or solicitor) may be needed.

Six to eight weeks after the application, the decision will arrive, under one of four headings:

- full planning consent, giving the right for anyone to put the land to the permitted use in perpetuity;
- temporary planning consent, allowing anyone the right to perform the specified activities for the period stated, usually between one and five years;
- personal planning consent, permitting only the applicant to use the premises as specified;
- refusal.

If the site is sensitive or the activity potentially contentious, a combination of temporary and personal consent may be given. Application can be made to renew temporary consent.

Temporary consent is better than refusal, but may constrain the enthusiasm of lenders, who want to know you can continue to earn so as to pay them back. It may also constrain your enthusiasm to renovate a building which you might occupy for only a brief period of time.

It is unwise to rely on a wink and a nod from a planning officer, still less from a councillor. In this field, believe nothing until it is officially confirmed in writing.

Any consent may have conditions attached. These may range from the innocuous, such as not storing in the open air or working after 7 pm, but others might be obstructive. If the latter, talk to the planning officer and explain the difficulty; he or she might be able to have the condition varied, or you could appeal to the Secretary of State (which is dealt with later).

Applying for planning permission

The formal system in England and Wales requires you to complete and submit forms, plans and a fee. Then the planning committee hears your case and decides, the decision coming in writing six or eight weeks after the application.

All that needs to be done, but long beforehand you begin the campaign. Planning officers (the full-time officials) and councillors (the part-time elected representatives) are busy people and capable of getting the wrong end of your stick. You need to influence them favourably.

To see why, start with the arrival of your forms at the local authority office. They are checked for accuracy and copies go to water, gas, electricity and highways authorities for comment, as well as to the parish council. Immediate neighbours are notified. Thus many people get to hear of your plans and to protest before the committee hears your case.

Most resistance is usually based on ignorance, misunderstanding of the true nature of your plans and consequent hostility. If that is all the committee hears, it would be natural for it to incline towards refusal. To redress the balance, you should adopt a particular course of action.

Contact the planning officer and invite him or her to the site. Explain your plans and answer questions. Describe your activities and show how small-scale you will be. With any luck, the result will be that official working for you rather than against you.

Next, the parish or town council. Do the same with them. Invite the borough councillor for the area and the councillor who sits on the planning committee for that area too. Call personally on any neighbour likely to be affected and explain yourself. Remember how important to all these constituencies the prospect of local jobs is, especially jobs for young people.

Then you are ready to fill in the forms. Immediately afterwards get every business organization you can think of to write to the council in support of your application. Now you can sit back and let matters take their course.

You may attend the planning committee meeting but usually are not allowed to speak. Nonetheless it is worth telling the chair that you are present should they feel the need to call on you for clarification of any point. You will hear the decision that evening and will get it in writing (probably with a number of conditions attached that were not discussed at the meeting) a few days later.

Appealing against a planning decision

An appeal may be launched against any of the types of decisions discussed here. There are two approaches: the written appeal and the public hearing. For your purposes the written appeal is strongly preferable, being quicker and cheaper. The appeal must be made within three months or you must have special permission for delay.

Complete the appeal forms and return them. The council gets copies of what you write and responds in turn, a copy of which comes to you. An inspector from the Planning Inspectorate visits the site by appointment and may ask questions. You may not question him or her but may only answer questions. Within 14 weeks you will get the decision, which is usually a common-sense one.

To appeal, it is important to have advice from a planning specialist. Ask about their record of success on appeals and get quotes for the work.

Leases

No lease should ever be signed without professional advice. Some negotiation may be required before a lease is in a condition that you are prepared to sign.

In addition to the rent, further costs are usually incurred:

- landlord's legal fees;
- your legal fees;
- landlord's buildings insurance premium;
- repairs during your tenancy;
- redecoration periodically and at the end of the lease;
- your surveyor's fees.

The last item is advisable in an older building to ensure that the condition is recorded before the start of your tenancy. Otherwise you could be required at the end of the lease to make good all sorts of dilapidation that took place before your time. For the same reason, take large numbers of photographs with the date recorded on them. A chartered surveyor will produce a schedule of condition for the landlord to agree to.

The lease may be FRI (full repairing and insuring), meaning that you have to insure and maintain the building to the standard in which you found it.

Rates and water charges

Uniform business rates (UBR) are charged on business premises by local authorities and water suppliers in a way similar to the imposts on houses. UBR are not cheap, and furthermore councils are forbidden to collect waste from many business premises unless they charge extra.

Rating assessments are not to be appealed against lightly, as appeals can result in the opposite of what is desired, a rise in the assessment. As with rent, accept the inevitable, recognize that competitors struggle under the same yoke and get on with doing things better than them.

CASE STUDY If there's a Polish elephant in the room –
burglars beware!

After more than two years of intensive development the Elephant Door is ready for production. And what is an Elephant Door? No less than a simple, brilliant but technologically sophisticated idea for premises security, fully portable and transferable from building to building.

Founder and CEO Radek Pallach describes its advantages like this: 'Elephant Door is the only security system that detects break-in attempts and immediately informs the user about the danger. The average burglary takes less than five minutes so the faster it is detected the more chance you have to avoid it.' Once Elephant Door detects a break-in attempt, what happens? 'A deafening siren (110dB) goes off, scaring even the most determined thief into running away.'

Traditional alarm systems take a day or more to install and require costly annual maintenance visits. Elephant Door, claims Radek, takes the property-owner less than a minute to install. Moreover it is controlled by a smartphone app which involves the neighbours, vital allies in the war against crime. For people who rent apartments, an increasing proportion of the population in today's mobile society, he sees it as the ideal solution to the problem of home security.

Even though it is only 11.5 cm across and 3.2 cm deep in a smart cylindrical housing, Elephant Door packs a powerful punch. If someone attempts a break-in on the door to which it is attached, the first thing that happens is that the built-in gyroscope and accelerometer detect any movement and vibration. Next, the programmed neural networks analyse the data in an instant, deciding if the movement is benign (for example, from someone slamming a door elsewhere in the building) or if it has the characteristics of a break-in. If it decides on the latter, the siren springs into action, delivering an ear-splitting alarm at the same time as sending a message to the owner's smartphone. To round off the picture, there's a key-fob control that programmes the alarm via Bluetooth.

The need to develop such a sophisticated product, coupled with the demands of getting it through prototyping, testing and into production, has created a number of jobs. Now 20-strong, Elephant Door's team are all specialists from fields such as product engineering, internet of things, mobile app development, design, marketing and business development.

The main problem that Radek has encountered so far is that every-thing seems to take longer than expected. 'We keep our focus on the business at 120% and do our best to achieve our goals every day – but some processes just need more time than planned,' he says.

The other problem is customers. 'People are really interested in the product. We didn't expect that there might be so many of them,' he says with a smile. That all takes time out of his busy programme, but it's an aspect of the business without which there would be no firm, so he knows he must cover it.

Having trodden the path that he has, from idea to a new product that looks set for take-off, what is Radek's advice to other entrepreneurs? 'It won't be easy. Be brave and don't give up!' he says.

www.myelephant.co
facebook.com/myelephant.co
twitter.com/myelephant.co

Key jobs to do

- Identify the sort of premises you need.
- Investigate availability early.
- Understand the implications of the Town and Country Planning system.

Managing operations

THIS CHAPTER COVERS

- day-to-day control of the firm;
- planning;
- safety;
- purchasing;
- quality.

Operations? You think I'm a surgeon?

'Operations' is the catch-all term for everything that goes on in the business, all the day-to-day things done to make it, er, operate. Managing operations therefore has two aspects: dealing with the complexity created by a teeming number of small things that are often interdependent; and developing a strategic vision of how it is all to be handled.

Once the overall vision is in place, you set up systems to deal with the detail. The aims here are: to standardize everything as much as possible; and to minimize the number of individual decisions to be made.

The latter is usually accomplished by creating routines, with rules and conventions for how things are done. Thus perhaps 95 per cent runs like clockwork, with only 5 per cent of exceptions popping up for special treatment, a much lighter load on people than if everything was dealt with as if unique.

The areas covered include for every firm:

- sales;
- purchasing;
- order processing;
- customer records;
- production;
- delivery;
- invoicing;
- payments in and out;
- stock control;
- payroll;
- staff records;
- financial records and reporting.

In particular firms there will be additional areas specific to the industry, activity or company strategy.

At the strategic level a decision needs to be made about the place of technology. Our ability to automate activity accelerates all the time, so the temptation to put in every bit of technology to do things cheaper is rising. But be warned by an ancient story:

> Dell made the classic nerd's mistake of underestimating the human factor – the first and last link in the supply chain – and trying to fill it with IT. As most companies do, it put computers in charge of the thing humans do best and vice versa, thus making everyone unhappy. (Simon Caulkin, Management Editor, *The Observer*, 18 February 2007)

The argument is not that IT has no place, just that it is unsuitable for the 'soft' areas where human interaction is needed. As Caulkin argues, these are those that interact directly with customers, both when selling and when delivering to them. I would add two more groups: suppliers and staff.

Plan before you leap

Planning the operations of your business is vital, yet some people resist it. Reasons include an emotional resistance to paperwork, a conviction that there's no point, since plans always go wrong and a preference for going and doing something useful instead. None of these justifies neglect of one of the owner's key responsibilities.

Some arguments for planning appear in the panel below. If you are not yet convinced, please consider them very carefully. If you remain unconvinced, talk these points over with an adviser to get a different view.

If you share my view, you will plan for each of the areas in the bulleted list above. If your operation is to be small, easily handled by a few hours' work a week by yourself and a part-time clerk, you do not have big volumes to consider. However, if you could find yourself handling a lot of activity, you will need to plan staff numbers.

For each area of activity from the list above, create a spreadsheet table that allows you to insert the time each activity takes, multiply it by the number of them in a day, then multiply them by 350 days to arrive at annual volumes.

Why plan?

- Making mistakes on paper is cheaper.

- When starting up you know least. Without knowledge, you need to think and imagine.

- Plans are always wrong, but preparing them makes you see important linkages.

- Even the simplest business is more complicated than it looks. No business can be planned and controlled in your head.

- After running for a time you put the plan right and set out on the new course. This teaches you why it was wrong. Without the plan you would not have learnt.

- If you don't have a plan, you don't know where you are going. If you don't know where you are going, any road will do. Some roads go to strange places.

- Thinking first often means you make or save more money.

Once you know the volumes, you can divide by the output of each member of staff, allowing for each full-timer 220 days at five productive hours a day. The figure of 220 may seem pessimistic, but it allows for holidays and sickness.

From the resulting plan will come the requirement for office space, equipment, furniture, parking spaces, restroom space and so on, for that particular activity. Repeat the exercise for each element of operations to arrive at the overall total.

Being in control

To control business operations you must know: what ought to be happening (from the budget and other plans); and what is actually happening (from your management information system).

To be of any use, the information you get needs to be timely and sufficiently accurate for its purpose.

Accuracy is desirable, but takes time. Speed is desirable, but can compromise accuracy. Think out, for each of your operational areas:

- what management information you need frequently;
- how often you need it;
- when you need it;
- an acceptable level of accuracy.

The information needs to be presented in a form that easily allows comparison with budget. The quality of presentation of information will almost certainly vary in different areas of the operation.

Table 8.1 Job card

JOB CARD	Ref No:	Description:	Order No:
Customer:	Customer Ref:	Plans:	Order Date:
Special Instructions:	Special Components:	Packing:	Delivery:
PRODUCTION RECORD:	Dept:	Dept:	Dept:
	Operation:	Operation:	Operation:
	Operative:	Operative:	Operative:
COMPLETION:	Start:	Start:	Start:
Target:	Finish:	Finish:	Finish:
Actual:	Time Elapsed:	Time Elapsed:	Time Elapsed:
NB: CARD STAYS WITH JOB!			Dispatch Date:

Accounts are likely to be computerized and so should provide management with comparisons of performance against budget immediately and accurately (assuming everything that ought to have been keyed-in has been). On the other hand, raw materials stocks may be kept on paper and staff might be lax in recording what they withdraw, so that a physical count is needed to see if the firm is about to grind to a halt. The armed forces say nothing moves without a piece of paper, a maxim that can be carried too far, but it does make sure that not many things get lost or forgotten.

Controls should start from the smallest unit and work outwards. In production, for example, the key document is the job card. It could look like Table 8.1.

The job card travels with the job through the production process. Thus, at any time, anyone can check on where every single job is in relation to plan, who did what to it and whether there is catching-up to do. It should be kept in a clear envelope and attached firmly to a relevant part of the work.

Its usefulness is governed by the extent to which people complete it, so you may need to keep an eye on that. Staff will be encouraged to do the paperwork when they see that their productive time is being calculated from the totals shown on the cards. Incomplete records mean they seem to be slacking. The remedy is in their hands.

When the week starts, summing up the cards will show what output is needed during the week, enabling detailed planning, moving staff around, asking for overtime or shifting some work into the following week, and so on. At the end of the week, review each job card to see where the delays were and consider action.

These checks will lead you to think about:

- extent of forward commitments and what should be done;
- spare capacities;
- scheduling of the next work to come along;
- holiday schedules;
- maintenance timetables;
- whether budgeted capacity is excessive or inadequate;
- scrap and rework rates;
- stock levels.

By this simple means you are on top of the production activity. If you apply the same sort of discipline to each of the other areas, your control of the operation will be as complete as it needs to be. It will never be 100 per cent, but it will be enough to reduce surprises to a manageable minimum at the same time as leaving you free for other work.

In planning capacity it is important to look at people as well as machines. People need:

- training;
- supervision;
- the right materials, tools and equipment, in the right place and in working order;
- safety equipment and an understanding of its use and importance;
- understanding of their work and how it fits into the whole;
- rest and refreshment;
- secure storage for belongings;

- understanding of the rules, why they exist and the penalties for infraction;
- decent treatment.

The real expert on a job is someone who has been doing it for a time. Learn from your staff: go round and speak to each of them twice a day, inviting comments on problems and how things could be done better.

Staff who have some discretion over how they spend their time can choose to chase the wrong target. Meet each of them for five minutes at Friday lunchtime. They should bring a list which shows:

- things they plan to work on during the following week;
- where they are now;
- where they plan to be in a week's time.

You can ask how they plan to tackle the things they list, using the opportunity for mentoring and guidance. If the list seems unambitious you can suggest additions, or if over-full, counsel a reduction. Above all, you can guide their sense of priorities.

The meeting is repeated every Friday, with a review of how things went against the plan of a week earlier as well as a projection for the coming week. You gain impressions of staff effectiveness and they get advice they need. You are in control at a cost of no more than 15 minutes a week for each key employee.

As signalled in the discussion of charge-out rates, it is unrealistic to expect employees to work productively for every minute of the day. You will impress on them the expectation that they will, exhorting their supervisors to make sure it happens, but in your planning you assume output for 70 per cent of the time you pay for. If you are lax it could fall lower, even disastrously so, but strong management should find 70 per cent a good guide for planning purposes.

Time you have paid for can evaporate easily, especially so from:

- poor punctuality, arriving late and getting ready to leave early;
- tea and meal breaks extending in length;
- time spent gossiping after a business matter has been discussed;

- smoking, popping out for 10 minutes every hour;
- putting business PCs, copiers and phones to personal use;
- poor planning, requiring trips out to collect supplies.

Control of these matters can bring useful rewards: you might need to employ one or two people more in every ten if you let them slip.

Spring-cleaning ought not to be an annual event. Clean and tidy workplaces tend to be safe, and are certainly more efficient. Make cleaning a task done at the end of each day, with everything put away and cleaned down. Neglect it for a week and you, and visitors, will know the difference. Keep on top of it and mess never becomes a problem.

2 Malaysia

The famous British cycle-manufacturer Raleigh Industries has a long and proud record of export sales. Over 130 years ago it began to trade in what is now Malaysia, becoming so successful there that in 1966 it began local manufacture and in 1969 was listed on the local stock exchange and began supplying the demanding North American market with Raleigh products. By 1980, though, government restrictions on overseas ownership brought the firm low and subsequent attempts to revive the name proved doomed. Meanwhile, over the years cycling had increasingly become seen as a leisure and sporting activity, requiring better-quality machines than the low-cost imports that addressed only that part of the market interested in basic transport.

Against this backdrop, the impending formation of the ASEAN free-trade area resembling the European Common Market of old, made business people realize that an enormous new market would open up, full of opportunities for growth, but also requiring growth for defensive reasons. The dash for growth gave impetus to local firms to seek out global brands and know-how. Montana Cycles had been in business since 1993 and had survived the 1997 Asian financial crisis, but in 2008 dropped its entire repertoire of products in favour of the Raleigh range. This sudden change represented, in effect, a start-up operation, albeit with ready-made experience of, and many contacts in, the industry. Their example is included here as the situation was not dissimilar in several ways to a start-up by an industry expert in any market. In the time that Raleigh and Montana have been together, both have been surprised at and pleased by the way in which each side's strengths have comple- mented the other's. The result is that Montana have captured for the Raleigh brand a sizeable share of the mid-priced, family- oriented segment of the market, the part expected to grow fastest as free trade throughout the ASEAN region takes hold and pros- perity spreads. It is also a segment with better margins than those at the low-quality, low-value-added end, which Montana and Raleigh are happy to leave to others.

So this is a tale of an enterprising Malaysian company taking a bold decision in giving up much of what it had worked for over 15 years in order to take advantage of an enormous new market opportunity (and avoid a major threat from new competitors) by teaming up with a firm of international renown.

www.raleigh.my

Safety

The Health and Safety at Work Act (HASAWA) requires everyone to work safely. It is worth remembering that it is part of the criminal code and that its penalties extend beyond fines to imprisonment.

While you will be duly careful for your staff and visitors, it is vital that you are even more careful for yourself, since if you were unable to work for a month or more, or lost some key faculty such as your sight, the firm would probably fold. Even if your injury were less onerous, life could be miserable. Ask anyone with a bad back.

If you employ people, even if only occasionally or part time, you need to give them an initial safety briefing and further briefings as new hazards arise, for example when new equipment comes in. Record its contents, get the employee to initial it and file the record. Be especially sure to require the accident book to be completed for any hurt, however trivial, and make sure staff know where the first-aid box is and how to use the contents. There are companies who will visit periodically to check that your first-aid box has the contents required by regulation and top up any shortages.

Before starting up, contact the Health and Safety Executive and check everything you are required to do (**www.hse.gov.uk**).

Purchasing

Purchasing can teach you a lot about selling, especially how not to do it. In addition to this free training you will discover just how many people make it their business to call on a firm in the course of a day, apparently believing that buying from them will lead you to a bright new future.

Buying on impulse is as bad an idea in business as it is in private life. All of your uninvited visitors want your attention until they persuade you to place an order. You will be unable to spare that amount of time and so must decide on a policy. Do you see everyone, but briefly, or see a selection, or nobody? The right stance will depend on factors particular to your situation, but it is a decision you will need to make. Remember that an oral order is still a contract, and never give anyone an order to make them go away.

For planned purchases in your firm the decision as to which supplier to choose falls automatically out of the process of specifying your needs. Whoever comes closest to matching what you want gets the order.

That presupposes you have drawn up a specification. There are of course two approaches to buying: thinking about what you want, defining it and searching for it; or looking to see what is available and buying the most attractive proposition.

Both have their place, but for serious investments that you want to work hard for you, the former line makes sense. It does not preclude taking a look at what is on the market first, to see what it is realistic to include in the specification, but the general principle of undertaking thought before action has to be right.

When buying, make sure that potential suppliers know about any special requirements. For example, if you have an order for a job requiring delivery of materials from the supplier no later than the 23rd, tell them. Make a note on the order form or include in your letter of confirmation a sentence to that effect. Not only does that emphasize the urgency, but if they deliver late and the whole transaction goes wrong and ends up in court, it may enable you to get judgment against them for the damages awarded against you.

When a sales rep completes an order form and asks you to sign, always check what has been written first. Ask for a copy before anything else can be written on it. Few salespeople are dishonest, but it is prudent to protect yourself. Keep that copy and check it against the delivery note and invoice.

Also, ask if the price shown on the order reflects the total cost. Usually there is VAT to add, but sometimes a hefty delivery charge or some other fee can dilute a saving you thought you were making. Ask for delivery dates, even approximate, to be written on the order, to commit suppliers more to keep to the salesperson's promises.

When buying through the internet the chance exists to print off a hard copy of the checkout screen. Do it and file as before. Telephone orders should be confirmed in writing either by the seller or by you.

All this may sound bureaucratic, and it is. But the advice is there for a reason: that many firms lose money, sometimes in quite large quantities, through laxity.

Vigilance is needed when the delivery and invoice come. It is wise to check immediately that what has arrived is what you ordered and that the price is correct, and to take up discrepancies straight away. Again, confirm in writing.

Quality

There used to be a view that people working on production could not be trusted to act responsibly and produce good work. To an extent it was true, not least because people were paid for quantity, not quality. Poor quality was weeded out at the end of the process by inspectors, a system that proved excellent at creating a great deal of expensive scrap.

Mercifully a more enlightened view now prevails in most quarters. Quality is not an extra, but is built into the product or service from the design stage on. Everyone in the process has a responsibility to see that their own work is up to standard and to draw attention to anything faulty.

What does 'quality' mean?

There are as many definitions as there are pundits, but most agree that it has to do with two broad requirements: meeting the customer's needs and compliance with regulations. I belong to that wing which seeks to under-promise and over-deliver and so over-satisfy the customer, but that view is open to criticism on grounds of cost. Furthermore, it can be argued, selling yourself short might make it hard to win new business. It all depends on the field you are in.

The management of quality is another matter besides. There is even a set of British (and international) Standards to cover it. Managing quality, brutally paraphrased, is matter of specifying the requirement, eliminating error and recording actions so that the process of production can be traced back if need be. And very useful it can be, too. If a turbine blade fails in an airliner anywhere on the globe, all the engines of that kind worldwide can be traced immediately and those with blades from the same batch isolated for checks.

In some industries it is expected that suppliers will be BS EN ISO 9001:2015 registered (details from **www.bsigroup.com**), but for most it is an option.

When a delivery is late it is tempting to skip the final check and get the delivery onto a vehicle. Consider the implications: which will be remembered and punished more, a few hours' lateness or a faulty installation? The answer will vary with circumstances but it is important to know what it is.

CASE STUDY Kenyans Mind Their (Business) Manners

Based in Nairobi, Kenya, Etiquette Xllent has high ambitions – to be among the leading firms globally in the fields of business etiquette skills development and executive coaching. Founder Eunice Nyala has set the mission as 'to empower corporate employees and emerging women leaders build self-esteem to help them stand out and enhance professionalism by projecting high levels of confidence in their day-to-day lives'.

Why should that matter? Ms Nyala has no doubts: 'What we do makes significant and fundamental differences to people's personal and professional lives – big changes that make people more effective in all kinds of ways.' To set about achieving those goals, Etiquette Xllent offers a range of services. Working with client firms and their staff, they create bespoke programmes to address specific needs In addition to addressing these specific needs, they also offer training and coaching in the generic skills needed by every firm, in public speaking, negotiation skills and relationship management. For individuals, they offer help in developing personal branding.

Recognizing that leadership skills are needed by executives and organizations, their Leadership Xllent Training programme helps individual executives to develop a personal leadership style. Unlike some other programmes, its strength lies in its personalization to the individual. As Eunice says: 'Because we don't impose a standard solution on everyone, but help the individual build his or her own approach, members of their teams can see that their boss is an authentic human being, not a programmed robot. And that can only make the manager more effective and thus raise the team's performance.'

On the topic of teams, Etiquette Xllent has developed another programme, Service Xllent Training, which aims to empower teams.

'If an organisation can get that right,' says Eunice Nyala, 'it finds that its customer service ascends to world-class levels. At the same time, individuals within the team develop and fulfil their potential. It can be very exciting to watch.'

Whilst Etiquette Xllent's training addresses the needs of the junior and middle ranks of executives, it does not neglect senior managers. For them, they offer services in executive coaching. American research has stated that the main reasons for using an executive coach are to improve an executive's leadership skills and to develop his or her presence. Both clearly affect the way they are seen by others. Again the theme of personalisation comes through. 'As everyone knows, each individual is different, has different strengths, weaknesses and needs,' says Ms Nyala, 'and that applies as much to senior managers as to anyone else. Some clients are naturally outgoing, energizing those about them; others are quieter though no less capable. In each case it would be foolish to apply the same approach to helping them develop their people skills. And we work happily with both the established senior manager and the more junior high-flyer.' Such work is sensitive – information picked up by the coach could, in the wrong hands, be used to do great damage – so Etiquette Xllent works with International Coaching Federation core competencies, which reassures clients that they are dealing with discreet professionals.

Coaching as an art not fully understood by all. The coach, a person of varied experience, systematically asks the client to reflect on his or her actions, which brings about over time a less instinctive and more rational and careful approach to the role. As time goes on – and to be fully useful it is a lengthy process – the client is seen to modify less useful personality traits and behaviours at work, leading to greater effectiveness and hence success. The process is planned to address specific needs and is delivered in 90-minute sessions, each session following up on what was agreed at the last meeting. Thus, as time passes, a track of progress emerges which, itself, can be a cause for reflection for both coach and client.

After a quarter of a century working around the world for multinationals, the switch to being her own boss represented a great change and was not painless. She now has to depend on her own resources much more, which is a challenge she has cheerfully taken up. At the same time she is wise enough to recognise that other views and perspectives can be helpful, so cultivates a wide range of networking contacts among her peers.

One aspect of the challenge is managing to deal with the inevitable ups and downs in demand, as clients do not form an orderly queue throughout the year. This has caused Eunice Nyala to develop three main strategies: to maintain and cultivate relations with existing and past clients; to seek constantly for new clients; and to keep her portfolio of services under frequent review. Thus she can return to old clients with new services to sell and offer an ever-widening range of services to potential clients. As it all takes time her watchwords are patience and persistence, and as she memorably says: 'Success is a process – the only thing that grows overnight is a mushroom!'

www.xllentcompany.com

Key jobs to do

- Calculate volumes for each activity and hence resource needs.
- Set up controls.
- Undertake detailed planning.
- Set up safety policies.
- Create purchasing specifications.
- Address the issue of quality.

09

Financial housekeeping, VAT and tax

THIS CHAPTER COVERS

- financial recording and reporting;
- banking;
- VAT;
- Income tax, corporation tax and National Insurance.

Financial records

Managing finance is of crucial importance, and is conducted with figures that result from aggregation of many detailed records. Therefore it is vital that those records are set up properly and maintained frequently.

The hierarchy of record-keeping runs like this, from top to bottom:

- no records kept, but all paperwork given to an accountant at the end of the year to sort out income tax, etc;
- simple DIY records, on paper or PC, enabling day-to-day management of finance;
- a bought-in paper system;
- conventional double-entry books;
- a fully computerized accounting and financial information system.

The first on the list may look like the cheapest but is far more expensive in accountant's fees than a record-system need be, but it can work for the simplest businesses dealing entirely in cash.

The second approach is the minimum needed if the facts of the firm cannot all be carried in the owner's head. It is often coupled with a variant on the 'two shoebox' system, where invoices payable are kept in a shoe-box on the left of the desk and those receivable in another on the right. In the case of cash shortage, a handful of debtor invoices are pulled out and phone calls or visits made. A variation is the 'four-drawer' system under which unpaid invoices are kept as in shoeboxes, but once paid they move to lower drawers in the desk.

The advantage with these systems is their simplicity and security: no invoice ever gets lost. Understanding the cash situation is simple; you know what is due to come in and go out by totalling the drawers or boxes. Combining this with records of orders placed (which

Figure 9.1   Basic financial control model: 'Six drawers' method

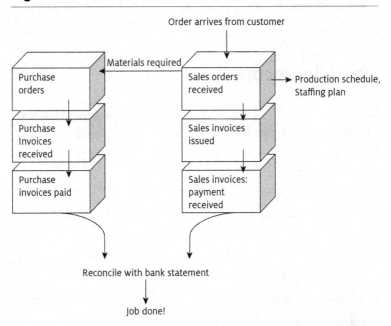

will have to be paid for eventually), the bank statement (saying where you started from) and chequebook (showing what has been paid but not yet gone through the bank) reveals the current and immediate future cash situation.

The bought-in systems, third on the list, can handle more sophisticated operations. Double-entry books used to serve mighty commercial empires until the advent of mechanical, and, later, electronic systems. However, instead of employing one of these you will probably jump straight to the final stage, given that:

- you will almost certainly have a PC in the firm anyway;

- the convenience will probably outweigh the cost;

- once the chore of inputting invoices is complete, all recording and analysis is instantaneous and accurate.

To take a look at the kind of thing on offer, search 'bookkeeping systems'. Sage, for example, offers small-business packages from £15 a month. They include invoicing and quotations, VAT, cash flow, customer information and more besides. This is not a recommendation of products, simply an example of a user-friendly site listing small-business software. When shopping, ensure that the software conforms to the requirements of HM Revenue & Customs (HMRC; **www.gov.uk/hmrc**).

Whichever route you choose, discuss it with your accountant before deciding, and build into your schedule a specific time daily or weekly when you do the accounts.

Bank accounts

Many sole traders operate only a single bank account. Presumably it suits them, but there are dangers in confusing the state of business and personal finances. If the account runs down, how do they know if it is because they are spending too much as a private individual or earning too little as a business?

Starting from the view that the owner ought to know what the position of the business is at any time, there is only one conclusion:

that there need to be separate personal and business accounts. Each account can have its own chequebook and credit card. Some banks offer charge cards for issue to employees for a limited range of purchases for work, such as fuel for a company vehicle.

Every week or month there can be either a standing order for the business account to pay over the owner's drawings to the personal account, or if cash-flow is unpredictable a transfer can be made when suitable.

Although internet-only banking is cheap, it is unwise to use it as the sole way of paying bills and receiving money. A PC crash or cyber attack could easily freeze the whole firm. However, some banks offer internet access to conventional accounts, which is a great convenience and offers the best of both worlds.

Tax and taxes

As this book has an international readership, taxation is dealt with in two ways: first, some general principles of taxation and its application, then the main specifics of the UK situation.

It was Benjamin Franklin who said there is nothing certain in this world other than death and taxes. This not being a medical work, it deals with the latter only.

Each country has its own tax regime, the guiding principle being to remove as much as possible from citizens' wallets, stopping just short of the point at which they go into open revolt. The best way of doing this, governments have found, is to take a bit of tax from as many sources as possible, rather than loading the burden all on to a single area. And they are very good at it. Very few members of the population are aware of Tax Freedom Day, the day up to which the government has taken all one's earnings for itself, and after which the people are permitted to keep their earnings for themselves. In 2016 in the USA it was 24 April, but 3 June in the UK. If it were all collected in that way in a single dollop there would be violent revolution, but politicians are too canny for that. Instead they put a bit on this, a bit on that, in the hope that either we won't notice or, if we do, we'll resign ourselves to it as trivial.

Almost everything gets taxed in one way or another, from the acquisition of aardvarks (in the UK, border inspection-post fee on importation, VAT) to zoo operation (more VAT, zoo licence, income taxes, corporation tax). The impact on the entrepreneur is both general and specific. In most jurisdictions the entrepreneur is required to pay taxes on earnings, on sales and on purchases, as well as on any employees; entrepreneurs in certain industries face specific tax demands, for example by way of fees for licensing or inspections.

In some societies the requirement to pay taxes does not feed through to an actual outflow of cash from the firm. Tax collectors may simply be inefficient, a taxpayer may mislead the authorities about taxable activities or, in some cases, a small percentage of the tax due paid over as a bribe may induce the loss of paperwork. Despite the pain of handing over so much of their earnings to the tax authorities, most people who live in those developed societies where the tax system is virtually incorruptible would prefer to pay up and enjoy the benefits of the rule of law and a general state of order. To rub salt in the wounds, businesses are expected to act as unpaid collectors of some government taxes. To prove that they do so they are required to keep records in a prescribed manner, which adds a further cost. At times, perhaps, they may be forgiven the odd wistful thought about life in the Wild West 150 years ago.

Not all tax is siphoned off almost imperceptibly, though. In the UK the self-employed face an income tax bill payable twice a year. Most businesses' cash-flow would require that to be saved up for, something being put by weekly against the day of reckoning six months later.

Politics plays a big part in taxation. Some aspects of tax are designed to exact vengeance upon a class of which the government of the day disapproves. Others are intended to incentivise activity believed by the ruling group to be beneficial. Most are designed simply to keep the government machine running. Thus, while the fact of taxes is eternal, their level can and does change. For example, at one time in the UK the top rate of income tax was 97½ per cent. It is now at 45 per cent. The Swedish author Astrid Lindgren claimed that at one time she was paying tax at 102 per cent of her income.

The UK situation

Readers unaffected by the UK situation may skip this section. Anyone who is unfamiliar with the tax system in their chosen territory could possibly find it useful to glance through, as most tax systems bear resemblances to one another, using it as a general guide to what to expect when they investigate their personal position in detail.

The authoritative guide to taxes in the UK, Tolley's, now runs to 45 chapters and some 20,000 pages, weighing in at 12.3kg. No entrepreneur should even dream of reading it as it is intended solely for the accounting profession. Despite its complexity in detail, the situation facing most entrepreneurs is simple in principle. That principle is dealt with here to the extent that the working business founder needs. Once the structure and requirements are understood, to assess one's liabilities information about the levels of tax and appropriate reliefs will be needed. Since some of these can change as often as twice a year, giving actual figures would be misleading. Consequently this book uses numbers only to illustrate principles whilst directing the reader to sources of up-to-date and authoritative information on the HM Customs and Revenue website which, mercifully, is thorough and clear.

VAT in outline

If you are already familiar with how VAT works, skip this section.

VAT is charged every time most goods are sold commercially. There are exceptions, including sales by very small firms and sales of certain 'exempt' products.

There are three rates of VAT at the time of writing:

- zero rate, in effect 0 per cent, on some food, books, newspapers and some other items;
- 5 per cent, on fuel and power, children's car seats and some construction supplies;
- 20 per cent on everything else.

The zero rate exists so that, should the government decide, VAT can be imposed easily.

Registration can be compulsory or voluntary. The factors involved are:

- acquisitions: business supplies bought from a VAT-registered trader;
- taxable supplies: goods and services rated for VAT;
- distance sales: when someone registered for VAT in the UK sells to someone unregistered.

The main reasons a business must register for VAT are if:

- its sales in the next 12 months are likely to exceed £83,000; or
- it takes over a VAT-registered business; or
- its taxable supplies, acquisitions or distance sales will exceed £83,000 in the next 30 days.

(These numbers are sometimes changed in the Budget.) An unregistered firm will be paying VAT on its supplies but may not charge VAT on sales. This is fine if you sell to the public or other unregistered firms. On the other hand, your prices to B2B (business-to-business) customers will be a bit higher, or your profits on those sales lower, since you will have to pay out VAT on purchases but cannot recover it on sales.

Voluntary registration was mentioned. This can be really useful to the small firm in either or both of two circumstances: it buys in a lot of equipment on which it pays VAT, in which case it can claim the VAT back; it sells mainly B2B, so that the cost to the customer is ex-VAT.

However, you do have to have proper VAT accounting and to keep the system going. There are provisions for de-registration, which can be found on the VAT website, **www.gov.uk/hmrc**.

It is extremely unwise to try to cheat the VAT system as the penalties include seizure of business assets, effectively closing the firm.

As well as sanctions and punishments for misbehaviour, HMRC has a range of schemes for smaller business aimed at simplifying VAT accounting and smoothing-out payments. The website has details.

The way VAT works for a VAT-registered firm running the standard system is this:

- Buying
  - Your supplier invoices you for the cost, plus VAT, say £100 + £20 = £120.
  - You record the invoice in your system as £100 of purchases and £20 of 'input' VAT.
- Selling
  - You invoice your customer for your price, plus VAT, say £300 + £60 = £360.
  - You record the invoice in your system as £300 of sales and £60 of 'output' VAT.

The VAT return

- At the end of the accounting period (which can vary, depending on the scheme you are on, but in the standard scheme is three months) you total all inputs and outputs and enter them on the return.

- Subtract one from the other and send a cheque for the difference to HMRC or, if the figure is negative, request a refund.

That makes VAT look simple, which it is in principle, but the actual operation and detailed rules represent complexity raised to the level of high art.

Income and corporation taxes and National Insurance

The Inspectors of Tax publish a useful leaflet, 'SE1: Thinking of working for yourself?', available from tax offices or online. It outlines your position clearly and they also run a helpline for newly self-employed people on 0300 200 3300.

In essence, as soon as you become self-employed you should notify the income tax authorities. You will then be required to complete an annual tax return. Your tax liability will be assessed under Schedule D, which confers the ability to offset certain business expenses against your income before tax is calculated.

No tax is paid on the 'personal allowance', which varies with circumstances. Until 6 April 2018, that is set for a single person under 65 at £11,500. After that and any other tax reliefs, tax is expected to be charged as follows:

- up to £45,000, 20%;
- £45,001 to £150,000, 40%;
- over £150,000, 45%.

Note that these are the rates applying to earned income; different rates can apply to interest and dividends (such as those paid to you as a shareholder by your limited company) and many more complications can be found online at the goverment website. Fortunately the entrepreneur does not need to know the detail – that is what accountants are for – but it is useful to understand the general outline.

In addition, you will pay National Insurance (NI) contributions in Class 2, a fixed weekly amount, and Class 4, a proportion of income.

For 2016/17 Class 2 is £2.80 a week and Class 4 is nine per cent of profits between 8,060 and £43,000. Above £43,000 you pay two per cent. These rates and boundaries change frequently.

Since Class 4 contributions and income tax are billed after the event, unless your personal cash-flow is excellent something should be put by weekly. After the first year the authorities will, to some extent, save you the trouble. Under the self-assessment scheme for income tax they will estimate your income in the next year to be the same and bill you in advance for half of the tax due. This, again, needs to be saved up for.

Corporation tax is quite separate. It is like an income tax, except that it is paid by limited companies on their profits, not by individuals. For the year ended 6 April 2017, the rate for small companies is 20 per cent.

Tax relief is worth a brief mention. Before starting up, check with your accountant how you should set things up to minimize the tax bill. Especially check with him or her if you plan to work from home, claiming a share of domestic expenses against tax. When you come to sell the house you will not want a bill for Capital Gains Tax which the accountant could have ensured you avoid.

Like individuals, companies are allowed to calculate their profits for tax purposes after taking account of legitimate business expenses. The website **www.gov.uk/hmrc** further details on a complex topic.

Net profit before tax	£5,000
Tax allowance (eg from buying equipment)	£15,000–
Tax loss	£10,000

You have not lost money; you made £5,000, but offsetting the £15,000 allowance has meant that for tax purposes you can legitimately claim a loss. You do not have to pay tax on the £5,000 profit as it has been wiped out by the 'loss'. Moreover, if you have paid tax in previous years you can claim back tax-relief on the £10,000 against it. Alternatively, the £10,000 can be carried forward to relieve your tax liability in the future.

This arrangement is subject to conditions. If you might want to use the facility, careful timing of your start date is advisable, as is the advice of your accountant. Tax losses may seem far-fetched but, given the generous allowances for any investment made in the first year, many new firms can make them.

CASE STUDY   Get past Canadian defences – if you can

Ever been into a building occupied by a business that's very security-conscious? You'll know the problem that Nymi Inc, of Toronto, Canada is tackling. Door after door is protected by passwords, keypads or simple locks, every one of which has to be opened by staff passing from one part of the building to another. It wastes time and saps morale.

Nymi was founded in 2011by Karl Martin to develop the Nymi Band, a wearable authenticator that uses the human cardiac rhythm (ECG) as a means to biometrically authenticate users. The Nymi Band enables 'always on' authentication in a wristband form that communicates over Bluetooth low energy and NFC to replace passwords, PINs and other biometrics to access digital and physical systems. Nymi's approach to 'always on' persistent authentication allows users to increase productivity through reduced friction, while significantly increasing end-to-end security.

Why should customers use the Nymi product? Karl Martin is quite clear. He says that the authentication industry, and cyber security in general, have been in a constant security vs convenience battle. The existing products on the market under-serve the market needs by making a trade-off that never fully satisfies the customer's needs. The Nymi system breaks out of that paradigm, allowing employees in a workplace to focus on the job at hand, rather than having to be in the middle of a mediocre (at best) security experience.

With a workforce now up to around 45 people, Karl Martin looks back along the path he has travelled. Was there anything he wished he'd known before he started? Certainly there was. He reports that Nymi has had to make a deep technology investment to bring to fruition its vision of 'always on' authentication. 'We have had significant market demand pulling us to fulfil this vision, but the time to market was longer than expected. Given what we know now, there may have been an opportunity to take a more incremental approach to both product development and market penetration to support a long-term roadmap.'

The present situation is far from trouble-free, Karl Martin says. 'As we have just launched into our fully commercial phase, the biggest challenge is maintaining a focus on the most immediate and relevant market opportunities. The nature of our product is such that we generate interest across a broad range of verticals and use cases. While the inbound interest represents great validation of broad market opportunity, we must stay disciplined in order to successfully bring such a deep technology product to the market.'

As someone who has taken his company from a cold start to its present size, does Karl Martin have any advice for new entrepreneurs? Most certainly. 'It's immensely valuable to constantly assess focus and clarity of strategy,' he states. 'As an entrepreneur, there are so many things that we could be spending our time doing, but without discipline, it's easy to lose momentum and spend time on non-essential tasks. Once a week, I will look at how I spend my time and assess how I can be more focused.'

www.nymi.com

Key jobs to do

- Establish appropriate financial recording and reporting systems.
- Set up suitable banking arrangements.
- Understand the VAT system.
- Understand the tax and NI systems.

10

Employing people

THIS CHAPTER COVERS

- people as a resource for growth;
- finding and keeping good people;
- recruitment;
- employment law.

People: the small firm's powerhouse

When discussing costing we noted that there are two major benefits from employing people: a reduction in the cost of a product and the ability to turn out more. Thus a firm that takes on staff can afford to reduce prices or promote more heavily, thus raising demand, and satisfy that demand through the higher output that the workforce can produce.

To take advantage of this effect the owner must recognize some key facts:

- People need special treatment.
- There are many similarities between individuals, and many differences.
- Managing people is different from other managerial tasks.

Anyone who has prior experience of working with people will recognize those truths (or clichés), but many entrepreneurs only stumble towards them through bitter experience.

Before taking on staff, take a look at yourself.

- Am I a loner who gets on better by himself?
- Am I gregarious or insecure and do I want staff largely for my own psychological reasons?
- Do I think the only way to exploit the opportunities available is to employ people, and recognize I may have to change to make it work?

The only 'yes' you should score is, of course, to the third question. For many business owners, evolving from entrepreneur to effective manager of people can mean quite big changes of attitude and behaviour.

Most entrepreneurs are driven people, always pressing for higher performance and better results. That is what entrepreneurs do, and it is right that they should. Too often their flaw is to assume that other people:

- are as driven as they are themselves;
- will respond favourably to pressure;
- are fundamentally lazy and need constantly to be pushed.

In some cases that will be true, at least in part, but in the majority of instances it is not only false, but behaving as if it were true demotivates people and makes them resentful. A resentful employee still gets paid, but, instead of directing energy towards the job, thinks of getting back at you. This is clearly not what you want.

So what is the attitude towards staff that gets results? There is no single recipe, but a combination of factors that are clearly present when people work well, and are absent when they do not. For some reason, in general, the British are not good at getting the best performance out of their people. A study by the University of Warwick showed that happy workers each produce 12 per cent more than their unhappy counterparts. Indeed, unhappiness caused workers to reduce their productivity by 10 per cent. Whilst you cannot control every aspect of your staff's lives and so are unable to guarantee their happiness, it is clearly in your interests to provide them with good conditions at work.

A large car-assembly plant run by British management had severe quality problems and was crippled by strikes and poor productivity. That plant was taken over by a Japanese firm and in a very short time was performing excellently. Astonishingly, the workforce remained the same: only the plant management changed.

The new management took a very different view from the typical 'top-down' style of management. They saw their shop-floor staff as partners in the enterprise of making good cars. They asked for, and listened to, ideas for doing things better, many of which were implemented. Instead of isolating themselves in remote, wood-panelled offices far from the shop floor, they visited the production area several times a day to see how things were going and took an interest. They wore the same overalls issued to production workers and ate in the same canteen.

The difference in attitude? In a few words, respect in place of contempt, springing from convictions that:

- the people closest to the problem are those best placed to solve it;
- management's motivational job is to set the course, communicate it, provide the necessary equipment and stand back, allowing people to do what they really want to do, which is to work effectively;
- management also has a responsibility to monitor and correct the course, intervening to clear obstructions so that work continues unhindered.

That is an approach that worked in a particular setting. Every business owner needs to think through his or her philosophy of management to suit the task, the context and the people. Once you have decided exactly how you and your firm relate to the staff, you are ready to move towards taking some on.

Extra costs and administration may be involved, once staff have been taken on. There is a legal obligation to offer pensions under auto-enrolment; there may be the Apprenticeship Levy to pay; and

the National Living Wage or National Minimum Wage may have to be paid. See: www.thepensionsregulator.gov.uk/en/employers
www.gov.uk/guidance/pay-apprenticeship-levy
www.acas.org.uk/index.aspx?articleid=1902

The search for good people

The military believes that there are no bad soldiers, only bad officers. Some might feel this takes too rosy a view of the perfectability of human beings, but it does serve the useful purpose of focusing attention on the role of the manager in getting results from people.

Taken to extremes, it would mean anyone could be recruited and turned into effective staff, irrespective of their past record, present ability or future aims. To dismiss that belief, as most people would, is to accept the need for discrimination. So how can we discriminate?

'Discrimination' is a word that has acquired undesirable overtones. Choosing or refusing people on grounds of gender, colour, nationality or race, religion or philosophical belief, marital status, sexual orientation, disability, pregnancy and (under certain conditions) age is illegal. The burden of proof falls on the aggrieved applicant, but quite apart from matters of principle, the time and trouble absorbed by even an unsuccessful claim make it unwise to place the firm at risk. The way to avoid the risk is to be clearly fair in every way you conduct the recruitment process, and to be in a position to prove you were fair. This implies written policies and records and means that everyone is put through the same hoops to test their suitability.

Put out of your mind any idea that it is your firm and you can please yourself whom you employ. You may not. But you are still, to some extent, the boss.

You may discriminate legally on grounds of most of the things that really matter in staff:

- education;
- experience;
- qualifications;

- ability;
- personality;
- skills;
- articulacy and literacy;
- numeracy;
- motivation;
- intelligence;
- likelihood of fitting in with the team.

Be aware that some of these could be interpreted as surrogates for impermissible discrimination. For example, 'not likely to fit in with the team' is risky, where the team is all black and the applicant white. Or vice versa. People might question your true motives.

The traditional method of discriminating is the interview, but research shows that it is a most unreliable predictor of performance in the job. Many experienced interviewers say they make their mind up in the first few seconds, one even stating that he chooses people on the way they walk across the room to greet him. Some rely on references, but not all applicants have them, some positive ones are written in the hope that they will help a nuisance to move on and some negative ones are revenge from an unworthy employer.

There is hope, in the form of the *assessment centre*, which attempts to mimic some of the situations the successful applicant will be faced with, observes performance and draws conclusions.

These matters will be explored shortly, but there is one more area to deal with under this heading: the process of finding good people.

It falls into a logical sequence:

1 Define the job in writing.
2 Define in writing the characteristics of a person who could do the job well.
3 Create advertising copy, choose the right media and advertise (or go to a recruitment agency).
4 Receive and shortlist applications against the criteria in the first two items above.
5 Interview and assessment centre.

6 Select the recruit, check references, offer the job and receive acceptance.

7 Decline unsuccessful candidates.

8 Induct.

The following sections address these issues one by one. Nowadays it is prudent to make sure that a paper trail exists to show that things have been done 'fairly', so while some of what follows may seem excessive, it is merely a part of wise management.

Define the job

There is more to this than simply writing 'SQL Programmer', 'driver' or 'clerk'. The job specification should include the following headings:

- job title;
- purpose of the job;
- post to which the post-holder reports;
- posts that report to the post-holder;
- location;
- duties and responsibilities;
- hours of work;
- special conditions, if any.

Job title is self-explanatory.

Purpose of job briefly summarizes what the job is for.

Reporting relationships: a family-tree type of organization chart can be used to express more complex relationships and responsibilities.

Location should include any mobility required, such as weekly visits to other sites, work on customers' premises, etc.

Duties and responsibilities are itemized and numbered, starting with the most important or most time-consuming and always finishing with the item: 'Any other duties that may be required from time to time'.

Hours of work includes any requirement for overtime, shifts, etc.

Special conditions could include any other important aspects, such as the need to have a clean driving licence, provide a serviceable vehicle, be ready for foreign travel, accommodate changes of schedule at short notice, etc.

Some firms include pay on job descriptions, but usually that is more conveniently and flexibly dealt with by other means.

Writing a portfolio of job descriptions covering all posts has a useful purpose in exposing any clashes of duties between different jobs.

Define the person

The person specification lists the qualifications, skills, abilities and experience of the person able to do the job to an acceptable level of performance. To create one:

- take the job description and cluster together any sets of duties that require similar characteristics in the post-holder;
- identify and list the work and life skills needed to carry out each cluster of duties;
- consider and record the educational or skills qualifications needed;
- consider and record the previous experience needed.

Advertising

Advertising costs money, but not getting the right applicant could cost more. It is important to:

1 produce an attractive ad;
2 place it in the right media;
3 have time, stationery and procedures in place to deal with an influx of enquiries and applications bigger than you expect, so as to look professional.

You may be tempted to cut corners with the sort of ad suitable for the local paper; remember it will be seen by not only potential employees but also customers and competitors. At minimum cost your designer should be able to create an appearance for the ad that stands comparison with ads from major organizations. You want the best staff, so look like the best employer.

If writing copy is not your strength, do your best but then get an adviser to review it and comment. It is important that the first attempt comes from you, rather than handing the task over entirely to someone else, so that you establish in your own mind what the ad is trying to say and can therefore consider critically what the adviser says.

The media to choose are dictated by the nature of the post. For a civil engineer you would advertise more widely than the local press, possibly finding you had to go no further than the Institution of Civil Engineers (which, like many professional institutions, advertises jobs on its website). On the other hand, advertising nationally for a receptionist would be wasteful.

Advertising on the web is now the norm.

The closing date for applications ought to be about a fortnight ahead. You will be asked about the date of interviews, so fix that too.

Responding to the effects of the ad can be difficult to plan for. You may get no applicants or you may be flooded. Know what you will do in the latter case, especially if it would tie up all the phone lines for a day or two. Nonetheless, response ought to be same-day, first-class post, with an application form and the job description, and any further information you want applicants to have about the firm. Insist on written applications so that, should there be any later dispute, you have clear, written evidence of the applicant's claims.

Examples of application forms can be found by searching online for 'job application form'. The results should give you ideas for constructing your own.

Shortlisting

Here applications are compared with the person specification. Those that do not show evidence of meeting major requirements are immediately discarded. The remainder are ranked in order of desirability against the criteria in the person specification.

Decide how many applicants you want to interview and allow between 20 and 40 minutes per interview, depending on the nature of the post. A further five minutes each will be needed to write up your notes while the memory is still fresh. Thus in a day of interviews from 8 am, with the last one starting at 6 pm, with 30 minutes for lunch, you can comfortably plan for between 10 and 20 interviews. Or you may wish to spread it over two half-days instead – interviewing involves intense concentration on each applicant, something it's hard to keep up. You owe it to yourself as well as to the applicants to be fully on form throughout.

Once the desired number has been selected they are immediately invited for interview on a specified date at a particular time with an offer to meet reasonable travel expenses and a request for immediate confirmation.

Interviewing

Before the interview you need to prepare six items:

- accommodation and a timetable for the interviewing day;
- a standard set of questions to be put to each candidate;
- an interview record and evaluation sheet for each candidate;
- an assessment centre;
- a record and evaluation sheet for each candidate's performance at the assessment centre;
- a grid on which to plot the results from interviews and assessment centres.

Preparing the timetable helps to highlight and address any scheduling difficulties in a complicated exercise.

The standard questions form the core of the interview for every candidate. They relate directly to the person description and the responses are noted on the interview record.

Table 10.1   Interview record

The Supremitude Company INTERVIEW RECORD			
CANDIDATE **J Smith**	**POST** **Sales Exec**	**DATE** **3.6.11**	**INTERVIEWER** **Jenny Bird**
*CRITERIA:	SCORE 1–5 (1 LOW)	EVIDENCE	COMMENTS
1 SOCIAL MANNER			
2 PERSUASIVENESS			
3 ETC			
4 ETC			
5			
6			
7			
OVERALL SUITABILITY:			
DECISION:			
ACTION:			

* Taken from person description

The records are needed both to aid a final selection decision and to create a defensive record in case of challenge. The interview record-form might look like Table 10.1.

You will need a similar record for the assessment centre.

The assessment centre itself represents an attempt to reproduce the jobs that the successful candidate will be expected to do and observes how well candidates tackle them. All the requirements relate back to the job description.

Using the example of a sales executive, the requirements might include composing a well-presented sales letter, making a sales presentation to a small group of people and dealing with a complaint. There would also be other demands, but examples are given for these.

The presentation should relate to a standard brief that you send each candidate with the invitation to interview. The brief (Figure 10.1)

Figure 10.1   Presentation task briefing

The Supremitude Company

PRESENTATION TASK BRIEFING

As part of the recruitment process for the post of Sales Executive, we ask each candidate to prepare a sales presentation of **no more than five minutes'** duration.

Each candidate will deliver their presentation to a small audience of Supremacy Company staff and associates on the day of the interview.

The aim is for us to be able to assess each candidate's ability to construct and deliver a sales presentation to a small group.

We ask you **not** to use PowerPoint. If you wish to use visual aids, a flip-chart on an easel and an overhead projector will be in place on the day. If you wish to use them, you will have to create your flipcharts or OHP slides in advance.

The brief to which candidates are required to work is as follows. Please do **not** introduce further product or market information.

*****

You are about to call on GalactiCacity plc, a large manufacturer of domestic appliances. Their response to the threat from the Far East has been to automate production fully, almost eliminating human beings from the production process. This is a preliminary meeting, following an invitation you had from one of their engineers at a trade fair. You expect there to be present representatives from their design engineers, production engineers, management accountants and buyers, and the chair to be a senior figure from R&D.

The engineer you met, Jim McLean, will be present. You have five minutes in which to persuade them that your company should be involved in a new development involving the use of revolutionary new adhesives in place of the mechanical fixings (nuts, bolts, etc) to hold their products together. The cost of metallic products, especially stainless ones incorporating nickel, has rocketed over the past few years, whereas chemicals have not. The environmental impact of a switch might be equivocal; there would be global savings in energy use, but an increase in emission of VOCs (volatile organic compounds). Use of adhesives would simplify end-of-life recycling. The supply of chemicals is less politically vulnerable than that of metals.

You think your case has significant strengths and weaknesses:

STRENGTHS
Energetic company
Good technical expertise in adhesives applications to hostile environments inc heat and wet
Used to problem-solving on joint ventures
Joint MD is technical leader in the field, having part-time chair in materials science at a major university

WEAKNESSES
Low output but could gear up
Narrow field of specialism
Neither MD is a good salesman
Up against major international firms
Firm only four years old

should obviously require a task that is not too far in nature from the kind of thing the successful candidate will be called on to do. To show the sort of thing you can do, a (completely imaginary) example follows relating to recruiting a sales executive for a specialist industrial adhesives firm.

In judging performance against this particular brief, you might look out for:

- a straightforward sales story; there are no whizz-bang items in the brief;
- ability to address sensibly a knowledgeable audience (eg they already know that volatile organic compounds (VOCs) are nasty);
- playing to strengths, like the joint MD's expertise, whilst acknowledging weaknesses with a positive spin;
- social points like knowing to pronounce McLean as 'Mc-Lane';
- a standard structure of 'tell them what you're going to tell them; tell them; tell them what you've told them'.

A superior performer would recognize subtly the improbability of getting the contract and GalactiCacity's probable motive of seeking a tripartite arrangement between themselves, the company and one of the international giants.

There is no obvious use for visual aids, but marks should be awarded for any instinctive attempt to use them. It is a good characteristic in a salesperson.

If this seems like a lot of extra trouble, consider that in no other way would you have a clue about how any interviewee is likely to do the job – until you have taken them on. It is a little late to start learning then.

To buttress the presentation, our sales executive should also conduct an 'in-tray' exercise, taking various simulated documents and recording on them the implications seen, priority to be given and the action he or she would take. In practice you would load the in-tray with many examples; in Figure 10.2 we show just a sales letter and a complaint. Note that today's date is 3 September.

Figure 10.2   Sample element of Activity Centre 1

> *From: MD*   *To: Sales Exec*   *Date: 25 August*
>
> *I shall next be in on 2nd September for a couple of days. Could you draw up a letter from yourself to Janet Jones at GalactiCacity, telling her of the new superpolymer and how preliminary tests show it meets their heat resistance standards? You and I need to meet them to talk it through.*
> *Thanks. MD. (Note to candidate: please draft this letter and hand in.)*

Figure 10.3   Sample element of Activity Centre 2

> *From: Switchboard*   *To: Sales Exec*   *Date: 29 Aug*
>
> *Sorry I forgot to tell you I had a call from Mr Durrant of Sierra Construction a few days ago. He was not happy with the latest stuff we delivered and wants to send it back. He shouted a bit. He says there are three lorry-loads of it blocking the site and said something rude about not paying for it.*
>
> *That's all I can remember. Sorry. I've been off sick and only just remembered.*

Assessors will be able to tell if the draft letter meets the needs of the moment. It must be done asap, given the fact that the MD is away after tomorrow and has already allowed a week for it.

In Figure 10.3 this one is both urgent and important. Three lorry-loads represents a large and expensive shipment. It is probably out of doors and at risk of being damaged by passing diggers, etc. Candidates should stress the need for immediate action, starting with some internal fact-finding: was the correct stock sent? Was it at the end of its shelf-life? Then over to the customer to establish the facts of the problem, probably involving a site visit at 8 am, and alerting a technician that he or she might be called to drop everything and rush over.

All of these points should be noted by the candidate on the document (continuing overleaf if necessary).

An assessment centre needs to be planned for and staffed. One person or group can witness and evaluate it for one candidate while another is being interviewed: candidates then change places.

Although the illustrations are of paper-based activities, other skills can also be tested in this practical way. If you wish to do this, insurances should be checked to ensure that cover extends to non-employees operating equipment.

Deciding

Interviews and assessment centres complete, you can now pull together all the results onto a single sheet. An example that follows on from the previous illustrations appears in Table 10.2.

You have now decided on whom to recruit in a way that:

- relates to laid-down criteria based on legal ways of discriminating between candidates;
- is recorded;
- will appear 'fair' if challenged.

Keep the records for two years, just in case. Then destroy them in confidential waste.

You telephone the successful candidate that evening to make the job offer, subject to satisfactory references. You write to confirm, sending two copies, one for the candidate to retain, the other for signature and return.

Take up references immediately. At least one referee should be a current or recent employer. They should confirm the post and its responsibilities, dates of employment, precisely, and at least not indicate that they are pleased to see the back of the person. Expect some guardedness, for conscientious people are careful how they speak of others to people they have never met. On this matter, when asked for a reference be careful not to over-praise an employee. If they are a poor performer, and someone employs them on the strength of your reference and they then fail, you could be sued. Best to confine yourself to dates and have a policy of making no further comment. Many companies do that.

Once satisfactory references are in, write to unsuccessful candidates thanking them for their interest and regretting that they have

Table 10.2 Assessment summary

Assessment Summary	Candidates						
	Browning	Tennyson	Eliot	Hopkins	Gray	Milton	Thomas
Score 1–5 (1 low) Interview							
Criterion 1							
2							
3							
4							
5							
6							
7							
Assessment Centre							
Criterion 1							
2							
3							
4							
5							
Overall							
Decision							

not been successful. Don't overlook this step and be sure to be courteous, if your first choice candidate pulls out you may have to go back to unsuccessful candidates cap-in-hand.

Induction

Work out a programme for the new member's first days in the new job. Hand responsibility over immediately they arrive, but shadow and mentor them until they are able to handle it with justified confidence. Expect there to be a heavy load of questions and supervision, but be patient; every bit of help you give enables the new person to grow. One day they will be able to operate independently, but it will not be in the first week.

Before they join, send matter to enable them to read themselves into the job and the company. If there are important meetings, consider inviting them as an observer. This person is family, now, and needs to feel like it. Remember that he or she will be anxious about their degree of ignorance and keen to perform. They may also have come from a firm with a very different culture from yours and will take time to adjust. That may lead them into early foolishness: if so, calm them, explain and forgive.

It is worth remembering that your successful candidate may have applied for other jobs and that a competing offer could still come through. If, in the early days, they begin to think that joining you was perhaps a mistake, they could still bale out, leaving you to go through the whole process all over again.

Example 3   **Canada**

In 2003 TDA Global Cycling (formerly Tour d'Afrique Ltd) was set up in Toronto, Canada, originally named after what was then the firm's then new cycling tour of Africa from Cairo to Cape Town. Ever since it has steadily added new routes, all on the same heroic scale, in Europe, Asia and America, springing from the conviction that cross-continental travel in a group, under one's own power, liberates the individual while developing body, mind and self-knowledge. Clearly, the eight people who run the company are experienced and committed cyclists. But their ideals run wider than doing just what they love. They are keen to encourage less athletic people to undertake their tours as an exercise in self-discovery, reminiscent of those great round-the-world sailing challenges for non-sailors. They also seek to pay back something to the far-flung communities whose lands, settlements and heritage lend the tours much of their magic. To do that they have set up the TDA Foundation, which raises money to give cycles to health professionals in Africa, thus enabling nurses and doctors to visit outlying communities, and people too ill to visit the surgery or hospital.

They used to run DreamTours, which offered keen adventure cyclists the chance to get together to undertake challenging escapades, usually crossing most or all of a continent. They still run cycling tours, but have now developed a new suite of products, labelled 7Epics.

7Epics is designed as a stupendous challenge, a series of rides totalling a staggering 72,000 km (about 45,000 miles) each of which can be undertaken individually, though a competition is developing to see who can be first to complete all seven.

When I was a boy, rowing the Atlantic was known to be impossible; then Ridgway and Blyth did it (we didn't know about the 1896 feat of Samuelson and Harbo). Then it was soloed. Now there is a race. Then in 1971 Fairfax and Cook rowed the Pacific. Covering the 7Epics on a bicycle must look to most people like an endeavour in the same heroic mould, but once it has been done something of the mystique of the unattainable must inevitably disappear.

www.tdaglobalcycling.com
www.7epics.com

The law: not as big a problem as some think

The law on employment can occasionally be, as on other matters, an ass. But for most employers it never presents a problem provided they:

- behave well;
- communicate clearly and thoroughly;
- know the rules;
- create and observe appropriate procedures;
- keep records;
- do not act in haste.

So far it has been assumed that the staff are conventional employees on the firm's payroll. However, hybrid arrangements exist and you need to be sure of the status of your staff for a wide variety of reasons. An excerpt from HM Revenue & Customs website appears in Figure 10.4 to help you decide.

Employment rights are many, though most are common sense and well known. The website **www.thepersonneldept.co.uk** is worth reading through to get a picture of all the areas you need to be aware of.

Figure 10.4   Employed or self-employed?

EMPLOYED OR SELF-EMPLOYED?

GOVERNMENT GUIDANCE

As a general guide as to whether a worker is an employee or self-employed, if the answer is 'Yes' to all of the following questions, then the worker is probably an employee:

- Do they have to do the work themselves?
- Can someone tell them at any time what to do, where to carry out the work or when and how to do it?
- Can they work a set amount of hours?
- Can someone move them from task to task?
- Are they paid by the hour, week, or month?
- Can they get overtime pay or bonus payments?

If the answer is 'Yes' to all of the following questions, it will usually mean that the worker is self-employed:

- Can they hire someone to do the work or engage helpers at their own expense?
- Do they risk their own money?
- Do they provide the main items of equipment they need to do their job, not just the small tools that many employees provide for themselves?
- Do they agree to do a job for a fixed price regardless of how long the job may take?
- Can they decide what work to do, how and when to do the work and where to provide the services?
- Do they regularly work for a number of different people?
- Do they have to correct unsatisfactory work in their own time and at their own expense?

Source www.gov.uk/hmrc

One important right is that to a written statement of the contract of employment. It must be provided within two months of the start of employment. The DBEIS gives a blank form that you can complete, on **www.gov.uk/government/publications/ employment-particulars-written-statement-form**.

If an employee believes they have been unfairly dismissed they can lodge a case with an Employment Tribunal (Industrial Tribunal in Northern Ireland) within three months. The period can be extended under certain conditions. To exercise that right they have to have been employed for a year – though there are some offences for which entitlement begins at the time employment starts (dismissal on racial or gender grounds, for example).

If an award is granted it may comprise two components, a basic award and a compensatory award, up to £14,370 and £78,962 respectively. Before the matter comes to the Tribunal, the Advisory and Conciliation Service (ACAS) at **www.acas.org.uk** will offer to mediate via their Arbitration Scheme (LRA Arbitration Scheme in Northern Ireland – **www.lra.org**). For the straightforward cases it is preferable, on both sides, to a full Tribunal hearing.

Entire books have been written about employment law, so here we do no more than summarize some of the key issues. It is an area that business owners need at least to be aware of, and preferably to have some familiarity with.

Disciplinary and grievance procedures are two sides of the same coin: one, where the employer wishes to take action over an employee's behaviour; the other, where the employee wishes to act over the employer's behaviour. It is a requirement that all employers have both, to a prescribed minimum. *Written disciplinary and grievance procedures are required by law for every employer.*

The procedures must have three features as a legal minimum:

- the written statement: a statement of the alleged misconduct;
- the meeting: a meeting to try to resolve matters; the employee has a right to be accompanied by a 'friend' (in unionized organizations, probably a union official);
- the appeal meeting: following written notice that the decision is thought unfair.

If you wish only to warn an employee, the disciplinary procedure is not invoked, nor is it for suspension on full pay. If you want to punish by deduction from wages, demotion, dismissal or in other ways, the procedures apply. These procedures must be notified to the employee in writing within two months of the start of the employment. For the sake of simplicity, most employers supply the documentation with the written confirmation of the contract of employment.

Conversely, the employee has the right to invoke the grievance procedure about any suspension or warning.

If an employee is guilty of gross misconduct it may be unwise to dismiss instantly. Instead, suspend on full pay and write later to notify your intention to dismiss and the reasons why. Offer the employee the chance to appeal. Use the time to collect evidence, information and witness statements to inform your case. Sometimes employers find that the employee was, after all, in the right, in spite of apparent misbehaviour.

Despite all this, there are grounds for fair dismissal. You may dismiss an employee because:

- they cannot do the job;
- their conduct is unacceptable;
- of redundancy;
- the law forbids the job to continue;
- some other substantial reason justifies it.

Nonetheless, it is still vital to follow the procedures.

Redundancy is when a job ceases to exist: the job is redundant, not the person. The BIS website (**www.bis.gov.uk**) lists 18 ways in which selection for redundancy can be unfair, thus laying the employer open to action for unfair dismissal. Most usefully, it also gives guidance on the safe process to follow.

For further reference the Citizens' Advice Bureau website, **www. citizensadviceguide.org.uk**, explains situations of employment difficulty from the point of view of the employee. The websites for the DBEIS, **www.gov.uk/browse/business**, and Business Link, **www.dti. gov.uk** and **www.businesslink.gov.uk**, address business concerns and responsibilities.

CASE STUDY Argentinians make developing-world cars into hybrids

Two young men met at Singularity University (SU), Mountain View, California, while studying on one of its programmes designed to launch new businesses. (Whilst SU is not the subject of this piece, it is a fascinating phenomenon in its own right: see **www.su.org**.) One, an Argentinian, Leonardo Valente, and the other, Javier Rincon from Mexico, worked together on their final project of producing a prototype solution to the problem of converting a normal car to hybrid operation. That original proof-of-concept prototype is now moving quickly towards a full-scale market launch.

SU's ambition – no less than to help solve the world's major problems – fits well with the aims of Leonardo's business, Exponential Motor Company of Buenos Aires and Bahia Blanca, Argentina. One of the key challenges facing the human race is widely accepted as the cutting of greenhouse gas emissions; the generation of electricity and transport in all its forms are the major culprits. According to the World Business Council for Sustainable Development, over 40 per cent of greenhouse-gas emissions come from light vehicles – cars and vans – so that seemed a worthwhile area for them to explore.

Many car manufacturers are progressively tearing up the old model of running a vehicle on liquid fuel alone, creating instead hybrid vehicles that run on fossil fuels as well as electricity, either using a liquid-fuel engine to generate electricity that charges batteries and drive electric motors, or switching between the two drives for optimum performance and fuel consumption. A few, like Elon Musk of Tesla Motors, have created a completely novel all-electric drivetrain, but at a price – in Tesla's case, upwards of US \$70,000 (£60,000) per vehicle.

Leonardo, who founded the company in 2014, sees Tesla's as a useful contribution to saving carbon dioxide emissions, but the price necessarily limits the appeal it has for the average driver. It is certainly out of reach of the vast majority in the developing world, where much of the expansion in vehicle ownership is expected in coming decades. His approach was quite different. Instead of requiring the car-owner to dispose of a perfectly serviceable vehicle and invest in a new one, he asked: why not convert the existing car to a greener form of operation? Having had the idea he went on to examine the different ways it might be carried out. All-electric operation, requiring large, heavy and expensive batteries was out: it penalized performance more than people would tolerate, he believed. Making the smallest number of changes would suit the customer's pocket best, so keeping the existing engine intact was his starting-point.

The breakthrough came when they realized that nearly all cars are front-wheel drive. That meant a new electric motor could be fitted to the rear wheels. If it was linked to the main engine, the car became a hybrid. This works in the huge South American market, but some of the modifications mean that stringent US and EU tests cannot yet be met.

Transferring the idea from the drawing-board to real life posed many difficulties. 'Batteries and engine performance were a special problem,' says Leonardo, 'as they affect the whole feel of the car to its driver. But we've got over many hurdles and are confident that we're getting there!'

The four-strong team at EMC – with skills in programming, electronics, engine design and engine building – are working on the product's next evolution. 'There are a few adjustments needed to the product, but only fine-tuning and ensuring seamless operation between the various parts of the system. It works well as it is, but we can always improve,' he says. 'After that, our focus will shift towards market development, but we don't want to be one of those firms who launch a product internationally that does anything less than delight our customers – we want it to be absolutely perfect before we reach beyond our home markets.' Will that take long? 'The product should be fully ready for market in, say, 2017; going global will take some years more.'

The lesson that Leonardo has learned which he feels would be of greatest value to new entrepreneurs is to be open about your problems. 'Growing your network as fast as possible, talking to other people about what you are trying to achieve and the challenges you face, getting their ideas on how to tackle them – it's unbelievably powerful,' he says. Isn't that risky – couldn't people just steal your idea? 'Of course, that's possible, but in my experience the benefits far outweigh the risks,' he claims.

www.exponentialmotors.com

Key jobs to do

- Think through your staff philosophy.

- If you plan to recruit, set up the correct recruitment, recording and employment procedures.

- Recognize that your main job is managing people, and learn how to do it.

- Understand the main features of employment law and set up arrangements with business advisers to help you to deal with them.

Risk management and insurance

Risk management strategy

To be alive is to be exposed to risk. The problem lies in knowing which risks are worth planning for and how to deal with them.

The business owner approaches risk systematically by:

- identifying those risks that could present problems;
- assessing them for importance, from qualitative (how bad things could be) and quantitative (how much they could cost) viewpoints;
- selecting and concentrating on the ones that would seriously damage costs or ability to operate;
- reducing the chance that the risks will materialize;
- reducing the impact, should the risks materialize;
- having contingency plans for recovery.

Such assessments can only be individual to each firm, but all will include the issues of what happens if:

- a key customer or supplier drops out;
- key staff (owner included) fall sick, leave or die;
- the firm ceases to function through an IT failure, fire, flood, etc;
- vital equipment fails or is stolen;
- key staff lose their driving licences;
- a major customer fails to pay;
- the authorities close your premises or the access to them;
- there is a regional or national emergency.

Many firms will find their list encouragingly short, but it is still worth spending some time thinking about the issue. Moreover, risk should be reviewed from time to time as the firm evolves, forms new relationships and, perhaps, grows.

As with coronary patients, so with small firms: the first hour after the event is the most important. As part of contingency planning, make sure that staff programme into their phones the numbers for:

- insurers;
- the local council;
- key customers;
- key suppliers;
- your security alarm company;
- utilities;
- the landlord;
- the neighbours, domestic as well as business;
- plumbers, locksmiths, glaziers, IT specialists, carpenters and electricians.

Keep an emergencies file at home, including building plans of the business premises that can be given to emergency services.

Involve staff in assessing what to do under various conditions and train them to react appropriately.

Prepare to deal with interest from the media.

Insurance strategy

One tool for reducing the impact of disaster is insurance. People often regard insurance as a necessary evil, buying the least necessary at lowest cost. That is not the wisest approach.

The new firm *needs* only a single category of insurance: that which the law requires and is therefore compulsory. It is *strongly advisable* to add insurance against catastrophe, as part of the risk management strategy. These insurances are discretionary.

Statutory insurances for business include employer's liability, motor vehicle, lifting tackle and pressure vessels. In addition, some professional organizations require members to take out professional liability policies as a condition of practising. Some industries, like travel, require bonding to protect clients' money.

Some say that catastrophe is not worth insuring for, as it is unlikely to happen. If so, insurance would be cheap. Since a catastrophe would, by definition, threaten the firm's existence, the small premium must be worth paying.

Many insurers offer bundled packages of policies for small firms, which can offer good value. They vary in cover and cost, as well as in the way they treat claimants, so shopping around is advised. All tangible property should be covered for full replacement cost (which could be a lot more or less than current market value) and the sums insured should be kept up to date. Otherwise there is a chance that the insurer will pay out only a proportion of a claim. Make a mental note always to tell the insurers of a change of circumstances, even at the level of having unexpectedly to use the family car to take samples to a customer. Without cover for commercial travelling, you would be driving uninsured.

The infallible guide to which discretionary cover to buy, and which to avoid, is the analysis undertaken to arrive at the risk management strategy. Its quality will be greatly improved if you involve a commercial insurance broker in the process.

Needless to say, insurance cover documents should be read with great care to ensure that you have the cover you expect. It is a tedious business, but very important.

Insurance suppliers

No insurance firm pays out claims joyfully with a generous heart, but there are some who are less obstructive than others. It pays to shop around, not just for price, but for the claims-handling reputation.

The best advice of all for the small business is not to buy direct from the insurer. Instead, buy from a registered broker.

A registered broker is quite different from an agent, consultant or other class of seller. Everyone else is out for themselves, or works for the insurer, but *a registered broker is responsible to the client*. In other words, such a firm has to put your interests first, in every way.

Not all brokers are the same; you need one who specializes in business insurance. Talk to a few, brief them on your plans and assess the responses. Ask to be put in touch with small clients who have recently settled claims as a way of taking up references.

CASE STUDY A healthy idea

Once upon a time someone said that a consultant is a person who borrows your watch then sends an invoice for telling you the time. Global Scientific Solutions for Health, of Baltimore, is a consultancy business cast in an emphatically different mould.

Back in 2008, Dr Paula Fernandes recognized there was a gap in global health programmes. Most companies and NGOs had general health systems expertise but lacked the very specific biomedical skills needed to provide laboratory testing to ensure diseases were diagnosed quickly and accurately. She decided to build a business that utilized her expertise in laboratory diagnostics and harnessed her network of international health organizations.

Once established, she found her clients requesting services that extended beyond diagnostics into clinical trials, market analysis and product development and has extended operations across 22 countries in three continents. Customers include governments, UN agencies (including WHO) and private businesses, all of them facing complex challenges and, often, competing priorities. They also work collaboratively with academic institutions involved in the same field.

All that complexity can lead to reduced efficiency and that's where Dr Fernandes and her 10-strong team step in, observing and analysing what is going on and preparing blueprints for rational ways of tackling the task. Not only do they impose reason on situations that may be approaching chaos, but they also have a wide range of specific technical skills that can produce immediate fixes. Like all the best advisers, they admit to any gaps in their in-house expertise and pull in trusted specialists from a wide variety of fields as necessary. Thus – unlike consultants who pontificate from a high level, leave an invoice then go away – GSSHealth delivers interventions in the field, a sort of one-stop-shop for both ideas and implementation that presents the customer with a complete solution.

The original focus to help clients improve the efficiency and effectiveness of health programme delivery has expanded from raising the standard of medical laboratories to analysing global data as a means of understanding and creating benchmarks for improvement. In parallel, the same information is applied to undertaking market assessments for new medical diagnostic products, which GSSHealth is well-placed to satisfy.

Asked why customers should use GSSHealth rather than a competitor, Dr Fernandes is clear: 'We are rare in that we span both the high-level policy issues and the practical implementation in the field, Clients like that – it means that their policy is seen through all the way to the end user of the service. Instead of ivory-tower ideas, they get solutions that really work or, if the policy isn't quite right, advice on how to tweak it so that it will work out there in the field.' She is alert to the danger of dilution of purpose on the journey between policy and implementation. 'It's a long road from the 85th-floor committee-room in a Western capital city to the health-worker in a village 200 miles from the capital of a developing country, a road full of obstacles and dangers, any one of which can throw a programme off-course. Clients can't know about all of them – that's our job, to see and understand the whole system and support all the actors in it.'

But doesn't that bring special challenges? 'Of course,' she says. 'It's one thing to have the plans, another to communicate them clearly, often to people whose English is not perfect. So we work equally happily in French, Spanish, Portuguese, Russian and Khmer. It's just another aspect of the need to be flexible and move quickly, with our focus constantly on our clients' needs.'

So there's a remarkable success story here, but it wasn't at all easy getting started. What was the main problem at first? 'Oh, finance, without a doubt. My credit card limit was $900 and flights cost twice that, so I ended up with multiple cards and having to pay in person at the airport. It was a ridiculous diversion, but somehow we got through.' Anything else? 'Where do I start! Probably the biggest headache, which continues today, was the funding cycle for big, public-service organisations. It can take up to two years to get a project off the ground, and we have to live meantime. That feeds into and amplifies the usual cash-flow problems that any company has. If anyone asked me how much backing they'd need before going into that area of work I'd say $200,000 or so, to be on the safe side. It could be 20 years before you are fully established. The other things that took me by surprise were the whole area of HR, the implications and minutiae of contracting and pricing. I mean, back then how was I to know how much I was worth?'

With hindsight, Dr Fernandes now sees two distinct paths she could have followed. There is the one she was forced to take by her lack of financial backing, and the other, quite different but high-risk path. 'Government organisations are careful and conservative,' she says. 'They like to do business with people they believe they can trust. Part of that is that they get to know you and your work, so that they know you are reliable, and part is how solid your organisation appears. To hit the ground running would need the $200,000-plus that I mentioned, supporting a team whose CVs are impressive. Even then there's no guarantee you'd get the work – hence my assessment of that option as high-risk. Even if you took the risk, returns aren't especially good and, with all the extra pressure on public-sector budgets, are falling all the time. Not only does that squeeze our margins, clients are taking longer to pay – up to a year in some cases.'

So, does Dr Fernandes regret what she did? 'Not a bit of it! We have a great team, some great clients and are doing useful work in helping organisations spend taxpayers' money more wisely to make the world a safer, healthier place for large numbers of our fellow-humans. A sell-out for millions of dollars after a few years might have been nice, but this is the wrong business for that and I get continuing satisfaction from the fact that what we do is so worthwhile.'

www.gsshealth.com

Key jobs to do

- Undertake a risk assessment.
- Develop risk-management strategies.
- Select insurance cover and suppliers.

Sources of help

What advisers can do for business

Good business advisers can offer one or more of the following:

- a strategic review of your plans, with comments and advice;
- a review of and advice on functional specialisms (eg marketing, finance, IT);
- technical guidance (eg employment law advice);
- one-off support (eg helping negotiate a bank loan);
- continuing mentoring to guide your progress.

Running your own firm can be lonely and exposed. Even when you have staff, you will never know for certain whether agreement signifies an attempt to ingratiate or a genuine opinion. Human motivation will always be in play, but advisers of integrity who are genuinely independent can offer a perspective of immense value.

There can be an issue of horses for courses as some specialists come to believe that they are competent beyond their own area. Equally, some generalists develop the conviction that they know a number of areas in depth. The only answer is to make your own assessment of the individuals and, as ever, to follow your instincts and take up references when you can.

Finding a generalist consultant or adviser

A good place to start is **www.gov.uk/business-help**. That will guide you towards Local Enterprise Partnerships and their Growth Hubs, which offer general and specific support and advice. There is also a business support helpline on 0300 456 3565.

There is also a wide range of local initiatives which, by their nature, cannot be covered in a book like this. Check with:

- local authorities (county, city and borough councils), some of which employ or fund business support activities;
- national governments in Northern Ireland, Wales and Scotland;
- Chambers of Commerce, which are often involved directly with government business support, but also offer their own services (they are strong in help for exporting);
- the local reference library: their staff know, or know where to look for, everything.

Operations launched by the Prince of Wales often address the needs of youth, but he has also created PRIME (the Prince's Initiative for Mature Entrepreneurs, **www.primeinitiative.co.uk**).

The government business support organizations in Scotland are Business Gateway in Scotland (**www.bgateway.com**) and Scottish Enterprise (**www.scottish-enterprise.com**).

Highlands and Islands Enterprise (**www.hie.co.uk**) operates in the north of Scotland and in the Islands. In Wales, **www.businesswales. gov.wales** offers similar support.

Invest Northern Ireland (**www.investni.com**) appears to operate under the full-service model, with advisers and consultants as well as a website.

The two national organizations that have never wavered are the Prince's Trust and Shell LiveWIRE. Both for entrepreneurs aged up to 30, the Trust gives advice, mentoring loans and grants (**www. princes-trust.org.uk**) and LiveWIRE runs training and a national competition (**www.shell-livewire.org**).

Specialist advisers

The main advisers a new business needs are a chartered accountant and a solicitor (both in private practice) and an insurance broker. In all cases they should specialize in, or at least be well versed in, small business. The best sources are from your local contacts, especially other small firms, who can recommend people.

Colleges and universities can yield surprising types of help, but it depends on local commitment, often on particular individuals with an interest in small firms. Technical and scientific advice is an obvious field, but there are also academics who study management, some specializing in small business. For the price of a phone call they are worth investigating.

CASE STUDY Book your space in Japan through an app

As anyone who has had responsibility for finding a venue for an event, be it a company conference, a committee meeting or a wedding will testify, it isn't easy. There are so many variables – location, size, atmosphere, availability, budget and many others – on each of which different stakeholders may have varied opinions. The search itself can take a great deal of time, followed by discussions, often heated, about which is suitable.

Tokyo-based Daisuke Shigematsu observed this problem and, spotting an opportunity for a new enterprise, in January 2014 started up his company, Space Market.

What does Space Market do? Mr Shigematsu's colleague, Haruhisa Saito, explains. 'We support event organizers to discover the best venue to hold their event by providing web platform (spacemarket. com) and concierge service,' he says. Exactly how does that work? 'Space Market is an online venue reservation platform that provides the largest selection of locations for all types of events where clients are able to search and book directly.' Since nobody can predict what the next request will be, variety and range are extremely important. Consequently Space Market's team of 30 have worked hard to tie up deals with more than 10,000 venues. 'These premises are available as our unique venue selections, including traditional temples, amusement park, movie theatres, and even a sailing vessel,' he explains. Once the user has signed-up to a booking, Space Market's concierge service takes over to ensure that the event is a success for both sides, thus ensuring that any problems do not derail the process and that users and venues are satisfied.

Space Market has concentrated not just on its repertoire of venues, but also on making the user's search, enquiry and booking experience as simple as possible. Their efforts were rewarded by the Good Design award given to Space Market for its iOS app, which works on Android and Apple's iPhone, iPad and iPod devices.

Chief among current challenges for the company, over and above the daily need that every business has of keeping the cash flowing, is that venues as well as users are not yet all fully conversant with the ideas behind the sharing economy and the shifts in commercial culture that it is bringing about. Globally, most aspects of life are moving in that direction, so the passage of time will probably take care of that issue.

Unusually among entrepreneurs, Haruhisa Saito has no regrets about his experience in launching the company. Asked what he wished he had known before he started, he replied, 'I do not have any exact wish.' He is clear about the reasons for his success: 'Because of our wide range of venue selections, our guests are able to find their best venue for their own event. Besides, our concierge supports their event-preparation to make it successful.'

Are there any other areas on which they are working? In a field like this there are always problems: indeed, if there were not, Space Market would have no need to exist. Probably the one at the top of Mr Saito's mind at present is the inevitable difficulty caused when, for instance, there are breakages which cannot be traced to a single individual. Who should pay? Should it be the person who made the booking – who may be entirely innocent – or should the venue build such matters into its pricing? Whatever the answer, Space Market does seem to have established a place for itself in the competitive Japanese business scene, by solving a problem in a way that is easy for the customer to use.

Asked what thoughts he would pass on to a new entrepreneur, he replied: 'I like the sentence "No challenge, no gain"'. He hopes that the world and governments will help entrepreneurs to identify and meet the challenges presented by an ever-evolving marketplace.

www.spacemarket.com

Key jobs to do

- Identify the types of advisers you might need.
- Locate specific advisers.
- Investigate public sector support.

13

After a successful launch... developing your firm

THIS CHAPTER COVERS

- is growth what you really want?
- motives for growing your firm;
- going about growth;
- your changing role;
- consultants;
- funding growth.

Your experience

Once the firm is established, maybe after its first couple of years, thoughts will turn towards the future. You will have been on a skyrocketing experience of learning. New opportunities present themselves constantly, many disguised as difficulties; the real problem is choosing which opportunity to take. Although everyone's experience is different, there are common threads, which will be explored here.

Key issues

If you grow the firm it will create hassle and involve further risk. Are you really ready for them? It is just as respectable to employ only yourself as it is to be the next Sir Richard Branson.

This is the time to decide what the firm is really for. At one extreme, it is there to give you little more than a job; at the other, to make you very rich.

Will it make you rich by founding a family dynasty, or by being built up to sell to a known buyer in maybe 10 or 15 years' time, or even five if you've developed the next Twitter. Whatever you want, decide on it, plan for it and go for it.

Being inundated with work does not mean you must expand production. You could subcontract the extra to someone else. Or put up prices to choke off excess demand, making very big profits as a result.

Doing the latter might change you into a specialist, high-quality, high-price niche operator, which might impose new demands on all aspects of the firm. It might also make you moderately rich for relatively little extra effort.

If you go for growth, recognize the key truth that *growing a firm is a different job from founding one.*

At a strategic level you need to consider:

- your expansion strategy – how you will actually go about it;
- developing yourself as a manager – acquiring the new skills needed to operate differently;
- consultants and how to use them – good ones can have wonderful effects;
- your mission statement – you need one, and it mustn't be waffle.

Expansion strategy

If you do all the extra work in-house you may have to:

- take on staff;
- expand premises;

- increase equipment;
- fund capital and revenue aspects of the expansion.

If you subcontract you must:

- manage the subcontractor(s);
- ensure quality and timeliness;
- ensure confidentiality (if relevant);
- fund revenue aspects (to carry more stocks for back-up, meet the extra cost of storing them).

Perhaps you do not have to choose. You might be able to begin with subcontracting sales or production, thus freeing your attention for whichever aspect of the expansion exposes you to greatest risk. The 80/20 rule might help.

It is a decision that will be improved by applying expert involvement. Call in a consultant.

Your new job

You may have got used to being the sole decision-maker on everything. You may also have done a number of manual or routine tasks yourself. That must all change. Your job in a bigger firm is to *manage processes*, *oversee performance* and *encourage people*. Other people do the 'work'.

Most entrepreneurs find this transition hard to make. Some even force their firms into failure by not even trying to make it. It is vital to recognize that, if you wish the firm to grow, your job must change.

A key element in success is structure. Allocate clear responsibilities to people and make sure everyone knows who does what.

You then delegate work to this structure, which then reports back on progress. You hardly lift a finger, except to inspire, monitor and mentor. In a perfect world it would run itself. Set it up as close to perfection as can be.

The three stages of growth

Stage 1: Foundation (you have come from here, but remind yourself of what it is like)

- Staff or contractors: few or none.
- Other people's tasks: minimal and menial, entirely under your direction.
- Your tasks: everything that involves importance and responsibility.
- Your knowledge of other people's tasks: total.
- Your focus: getting the work in, getting the jobs out, collecting payment.
- Structure: wheel-shaped, with you as the hub and everyone else looking to you.

Stage 2: Development (where you may be, or may be headed, at present)

- Staff or contractors: 5 to 50 (approximately).
- Other people's tasks: specialized but still under your direction, either directly or via a supervisor.
- Your tasks: still carrying overall responsibility and requiring others to do things your way.
- Your knowledge of other people's tasks: variable – limited in some cases to a general view, total in others.
- Your focus: getting the work in, getting the jobs out, getting payment, staff management.
- Structure: a pyramid, with you firmly at the top.

Stage 3: Delegation (where you want to be)

- Staff or contractors: 50 (approximately) upwards to thousands.
- Other people's tasks: specialized, delivering their small part of the big jigsaw.

- Your tasks: still carrying overall responsibility but unable to exercise direct leadership of the workforce. Now operating entirely through intermediary managers or supervisors.

- Your knowledge of other people's tasks: highly variable and constantly falling as far as the mundane is concerned, growing in the case of the challenges facing your subordinate managers.

- Your focus: the business environment, key customer and supplier relationships, company culture, managing and developing your managers.

- Structure: the traditional organization chart or, in some cases, a soft systems diagram (there's no space here to go into what that is, but if you know the jargon you'll recognize it; if you don't, it's not important).

It is obvious that Stage 3 is different from its predecessors. If the firm is to grow effectively you must complete the journey to Stage 3.

You might have the skills already to work well at Stage 3; your skills might evolve through experience or you might want to take training. There is an enormous variety of training available; time is precious; so there is no reason to buy any that is not exactly what you want.

Organizational culture

This matter was tucked away under 'your focus' in the description of Stage 3 above. It is not dealt with elsewhere in this book. So what is it and why is it important?

'Culture' is hard to define, but easy to spot when you see it. It is 'the way we do things round here'. It is in the atmosphere of the place. It shows in the way people deal with each other. It shows in attitudes to customers and suppliers. It is probably the main factor in retaining good people – which, along with customers and finances, will become your main preoccupation.

You set the most important example in the firm. You show the standard of behaviour, the level of integrity, the way of addressing people that becomes the norm. Staff will watch and copy you, so if you want them to be the sort of people your customers, suppliers and colleagues would be happy to deal with, be that sort of person yourself. There is no room for double standards, no place for 'do as I say, not as I do'.

Your managerial development

Management is complex. Expansion complicates it further. To deal effectively with it requires learning. Not all of what you need to learn is taught at Business School.

Learning involves change and humans do not like change, so it is not easy. Read when you get the chance (the library shelf number for management is 658), and you will find extraordinary insights from some great minds. The internet is another obvious source, but recognize that a major element in learning is direct interaction face-to-face with others.

Your firm and consultants

Consultants, they say, borrow your watch to tell you the time, then keep the watch. Whatever the truth of that, the good ones are worth a lot of Rolexes. The only way a consultant can stay in business is: either to fleece a constant procession of single-use clients, or deliver real satisfaction and value, remaining in constant demand.

It often comes as a surprise to entrepreneurs how much a good consultant knows about the firm before setting a foot in the door. That comes about through study and thought. As a result, they ought to be up to date with everything in their field, so they save your precious time. Further, you may be too close to the situation to see it clearly.

How do you tell a good consultant from the others? Common sense dictates asking for several examples of past work and permission to contact those clients. The obvious expedient of going to one of the big firms may not be your best plan. Few of them have seen a small firm and understand the pressures on you, and some may work to a formula designed as much to minimize the risk of successful lawsuits as to help the client. Nevertheless, they do employ some bright people, so do not automatically dismiss them.

Funding your growth

Many growing firms find that expansion plans are thwarted by exhausting their capacity to raise more loan capital. This need not be the bank acting difficult; for perfectly proper reasons, it is wrong to get the balance between loan and equity (the owners' fixed capital) too far out of kilter. Conventional wisdom says a pound of loan should be matched by a pound of equity.

Most small firms are financed by arrangements to put that formula in the shade. That is usually because there is hidden equity, in the form of a bank lien on the owner's house, behind the loans.

When the day comes that more funding is required than can be supported, assuming that the owners have no personal source of funds they want to invest, the firm will need to become a limited company and sell shares. The high street banks do not buy shares in small firms. That is done by private individuals or investment banks.

Most investment banks are not interested in investing the odd million or two, but there are specialist firms who are keen to consider such opportunities. Their motives are simple and clear. They want to be able to sell their shares within only a few years for a greatly inflated price.

The investment bank will press you hard for performance. It does not mind who it sells to as long as their money is good. You, on the other hand, might mind a great deal.

On the other hand, you may choose to grow with support from one of the newer sources of finance, business angels. P2P lenders and investors and crowdfunders may not resemble traditional financiers, but they will impose their own disciplines, demands and pressures.

CASE STUDY Business coach needed a business coach

In 2014, after 21 years as an entrepreneur, Rivers Corbett MBA decided the time had come to pass on to the next generation the lessons he had learned, by setting up a business-coaching consultancy. He confesses there was something missing from his life. 'What I needed most of all was a business coach, someone to ask the right questions to make me concentrate on the important things; that kind of tough love can be so powerful,' he says.

A year later he felt he'd not only got his business proposition sorted, but, in addition, had learned how valuable his services could be to his clients. 'If someone could have done for me what I do for them I would have been so much more effective, so much sooner,' he claims.

Confident that he'd designed a system that would be an effective basis for running both his own business and for his clients to adopt, Rivers, based in New Brunswick, Canada, had his eyes focused firmly on the job his company does, helping business coaches and start-ups to find clients. 'Once a coach has a track record, it's a lot easier to convince new clients to give him or her a chance,' he says, 'but when you're starting out there's quite a mountain to climb.'

Where does Rivers get his confidence that he has anything to offer? Well, StartUP Canada gave him its StartUP Champion Award. Also he's won *Profit* Magazine's 2015 Business Person of the Year and appears on its list of hottest start-ups as well as its list of Canada's fastest-growing companies. *Profit* Magazine has been going since 1982 and probably knows a good thing when it sees it.

Deeply involved in the entrepreneurial movement in his Province and his country, Rivers helped found StartUP Canada and hosts its podcast show (**www.startupcan.ca/podcasts**). The Opportunities New Brunswick team is another of Rivers's involvements and boasts of the Province's advantages over east-coast USA as a business location: nothing if not ambitious.

So here is a man who networks widely among the very people in a position to put business his way and proves his credentials as a human being by taking on responsibilities of social value. But all that has to be paid for, and Rivers's main income is from Coaching by RockSTARs which advises business coaches in 24 countries. In parallel, the RockSTAR StartUP Academy aims to help new entrepreneurs to increase their chances of success. In addition he co-founded rayZen Innovations, a firm that helps the charitable and not-for-profit sector to improve its performance.

As for Coaching by RockSTARS, why should customers decide to work with it rather than one of its many competitors? Rivers is emphatic: 'Our approach offers three key advantages: first, clients learn how to get all the business leads they need without putting prospects off by sounding like salespeople; second, they understand how to convert those leads into long-term client relationships; third, they see how to get real results for clients, irrespective of business type, industry or country.'

Unsurprisingly, perhaps, given the breadth of his activities, Rivers sees his biggest problem currently as one of balance. But, as a coach, he is equipped to deal with it. As he would tell his clients, it is all about establishing the right priorities at any one time and sticking to them.

His advice for the new entrepreneur is characteristically simple: 'It's a *great* game but make sure you know and practise the rules for success.'

Website: www.coachingbyrockstars.com

Key jobs to do

- Decide if expansion really is for you.
- Decide the strategy for carrying it out.
- Understand the nature of your new job.
- Decide on what culture you should encourage within the firm.
- Create a programme for developing yourself as a manager.
- Select a strategy for using consultants.
- Recognize the implications of selling shares to fund growth.

14

The PLG Programme for Growth

The PLG Programme: Prepare, Launch, Grow©

The PLG Programme leads you step by step through the process of:

- preparation… for setting-up your business on firm foundations;
- launch… of the firm on the right lines;
- growth… to fulfil your potential.

More than half of new firms fail in their first few years. More fail when they try to grow. Usually it is because of poor planning, which can be avoided.

The PLG Programme helps you build a robust business plan, methodically directing you to the right parts of *Starting a Successful Business* as well as to outside resources.

Start your new business here…

> **The PLG Programme:**
> **Prepare, Launch, Grow**

What it's for

The overall aim is to end up with a complete business plan for your new firm.

Preparing a business plan helps you by making your mistakes the cheap way – on paper. It helps banks to see what you want to borrow and why. It gives you a standard against which to measure progress.

You will need access to:

- a copy of *Starting a Successful Business*, 8th edition;
- a PC with broadband connection;
- a telephone;
- a spreadsheet and word processor.

What follows might look daunting at first, but just do one thing after another and you will get to the end.

How it works

The instructions are divided into the three PLG sections, reflecting the stages of your business: Prepare, Launch, Grow.

Within each section are subheadings. Under each subheading is, where appropriate, a direction to the chapter of *Starting a Successful Business* which is relevant. The subheading tells you what you have to write for that part of your business plan and the book gives the necessary background.

After a time you will find you are making real progress towards the goal and, eventually, you will end up with a complete business plan. That plan is mainly for you, to make sure you have thought about tying all the components of your firm together, but it will also be ready for the bank, to support your case for borrowing.

Next...

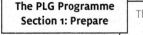

The PLG Programme
Section 1: Prepare

The PLG Programme
Section 2: Launch

The PLG Programme
Section 3: Grow

Business plan: introduction

Executive summary

This is where you summarize the plan briefly. The idea is to give the reader a picture of the complete proposal before they launch into the detail.

As it is a summary of the plan, you have to write the plan first!

Once the plan is finished, return here and write the executive summary. It should be no longer than three paragraphs and should give just the main features of the business. It should be sober and sensible, not shouting or screaming with enthusiasm. The people who will read it have seen business plans come and go. They would not be impressed.

Now that we have started to think about writing, consider what style is best. My suggestion is that you:

- use a direct, clear type of English (which I am aiming for here);
- use short words and simple language;
- keep sentences short, one thought per sentence;
- keep paragraphs short, one argument per paragraph;
- use bullet-point lists when appropriate;
- make the main points well, but don't try to answer every potential question;
- number the pages;
- put any large mass of detail into an appendix, at the end.

Where people might want to refer in discussion to specific points, it helps if you number the relevant paragraphs or items in lists.

And when you have finished the plan, get someone who does not know the industry to read it, to see if it makes sense to them. Most official readers will not understand your industry either.

Next…

Business plan: Part one: Overviews

Business overview

Here you describe what the business as a whole is to do, your vision for it. It should take a paragraph, maybe three to five sentences.

If it's not clear what is needed, imagine bumping into a friend in the street. Both of you are in a hurry but want to be polite. They say: 'This business of yours. What's the idea behind it? Where does it fit in?'

You might answer: 'It's the only Polish restaurant for 30 miles; the cooks and staff will all be Polish and we'll offer families an affordable home-cooking alternative to the usual curry or chow mein. When the first one's got going I'll open another in the next town, and so on. Polish expats will love it and the Brits will too.'

In three sentences the vision for the business has been described. Word it a bit more formally, and it is suitable for the bank, or anyone. The bank would put the question more bluntly: 'What makes you think this idea will work?' So answer them. You already have, almost.

Expect to come back here to make changes as the plan evolves. The headings of the plan itself follow. Under each heading, where it applies, is given the relevant chapter of *Starting a Successful Business*.

Business background

Summarize only, giving notes on the main points. Bullet-points are fine.

Principals

Who you are – qualifications, background, experience.

Start date

When you plan to start.

Present position

How far you have got.

Business identity

Legal constitution, business name, trading name. See: Chapter 5, *Your business name and legal status.*

Market background

See: Chapter 2, *Getting orders, making profits.*

The industry

The industry at present – structure, customers, suppliers, distribution system.

Unique proposition

Why customers will want to come to you – the benefits you offer.

Market information

Market size, history, important issues and likely direction of development.

Present suppliers to the market

How customer needs are met at present, who competitors are, their methods and the share each holds (these can be estimated, in which case say so).

Market developments

What you expect to happen and how suppliers and competitors are likely to respond.

The PLG Programme
Section 1: Prepare

The PLG Programme
Section 2: Launch

The PLG Programme
Section 3: Grow

Business plan: Part two: Operating plans

Marketing plans

Here you describe things in more detail. A balance needs to be struck between keeping it brief yet giving enough information. If tempted to write too much, remember you usually have a chance to answer questions face to face. See: Chapter 2, *Getting orders, making profits.*

Positioning

How your service or product will be positioned against competition.

Sales proposition

Why the customer should buy from you.

Target customers

Analyse the market, specify the group you will aim at, say how many of them there are and where.

Pricing

Define your approach to pricing and relate it to your sales proposition.

Sales operations

How you will contact and sell to customers, who will do it, how many orders a week this should produce and their value.

Promotion

How you will support the sales effort and attract enquiries.

Distribution

By which channel(s) the product will reach the customer.

After-sales

Any special follow-up or opportunities to sell maintenance, etc.

Operating plans

See: Chapter 1, *First thoughts and foundations*; Chapter 2, *Getting orders, making profits*; Chapter 7, *Premises*; Chapter 8, *Managing operations*; Chapter 9, *Financial housekeeping, VAT and tax*; Chapter 10, *Employing people*; Chapter 11, *Risk management and insurance*.

Production

How what you sell is to be produced, maximum output capacity and how it compares with sales forecasts, longer-term plans.

Premises

Plans for accommodation, how satisfactory it is, tenure, longer-term plans.

Administration

How you will handle enquiries, orders, sales, invoices, accounts, stock, personnel.

Information systems

How stock will be controlled, how accounting information for management will be produced and when, how they will cope with growth.

IT

What IT you plan to acquire, how, why, who will operate it, arrangements for maintenance and support.

Sales forecast

Monthly for the first two years, annually for the next three.

Financial plans

This is part commentary, part tables. Your accountant should check your work first.

See: Chapter 3, *Controlling the money*; Chapter 4, *Raising the money*.

Capital requirements

The money needed to get the business going on a sound financial basis, divided into fixed capital (for long-term purchases) and working capital (to cover day-to-day fluctuations in cash flow).

Financing strategy

Where the money will come from, security offered, repayment period. If a limited company, how much in shares and how much on loan.

Cash-flow projection

Monthly, covering the first two years.

Profit-and-loss projection

Annually, covering the first five years.

The PLG Programme **Section 1: Prepare**	The PLG Programme Section 2: Launch	The PLG Programme Section 3: Grow

Business plan: Part three: Appendices

An appendix is where you put the indigestible lumps of information that have to be present, but are too detailed or fussy for the main document. It is up to you to judge what to include or exclude here. The main document may refer to the appendix where necessary.

A curriculum vitae (CV) for each of the principals in the firm is essential, and is best placed as an appendix. Detailed product costings might appear here, too. Each appendix should be numbered.

That's it! You have now completed your business plan... except for one small point. You need to go back and write the executive summary at the beginning.

Business plan: Presentation

To make the best impression:

- Use white paper, selecting a font of 12pt (certainly no less than 10pt) for the main text.

- Don't use colour or fancy effects: they do not impress and can delay or obstruct download if you send it as an e-mail attachment.

- Start with a title page, giving names, contact numbers and e-mail addresses and prominently featuring the word CONFIDENTIAL.

- Next, have a contents page.

- Check carefully for spelling and grammar; be sure that the different pieces are consistent with each other; have others read it to make sure it is quite clear.

- Put it in a cover that can easily be removed by the recipient for copying.

Once you are ready, you can move to Section 2, the launch phase of your business...

The PLG Programme Section 1: Prepare	**The PLG Programme Section 2: Launch**	The PLG Programme Section 3: Grow

Business plan: Implementation

In Section 2 of the Programme you put your plans into practice.

Draw up a programme for implementing your plans, based on the written business plan you completed earlier, in Section one of the PLG Programme.

Start first on whatever will take longest to complete. Since everybody's programmes vary, there is no general pattern to offer you. You will need to put the items in your business plan into the order that makes most sense in your unique situation.

Put your programme into practice, keeping a strict eye on everything. Remember that, even though you put a lot into it, your business plan is only a plan. It is guaranteed to be wrong. So look out for deviations and correct them as soon as they happen. That way you should stay on course.

If your plan is badly out, tell anyone who needs to know and rewrite it.

Once the firm is up and running, keep on top of things by watching the measures you have put in place.

Report regularly how things are going to those who need to know.

Involve advisers and listen to their views. If they give you bad news, that is what you most need to hear.

See: all of *Starting a Successful Business*.

Once the company is running well, you may want to plan for further growth. That is addressed in the final part of the PLG Programme...

Business plan: Growth

You have decided to grow, or at least to plan for growth and see what the implications are.

If it sounds strange to do all that work, and then decide not to grow, remember that it is perfectly possible to find that growth at this moment will mean, for example, taking on unacceptably large loans, or require skills that your staff do not have. Only planning will reveal those facts.

The method followed is to repeat the business plan headings used earlier for the new firm, but with changes to reflect the fact that you now have a history. For that reason some of what follows may seem familiar.

The growth plan starts here...

| The PLG Programme | | |
| Section 1: Prepare | | |

| The PLG Programme | |
| Section 2: Launch | |

| **The PLG Programme** |
| **Section 3: Grow** |

Executive summary

This is where you summarize the plan briefly. The idea is to give the reader a picture of the complete proposal before they launch into the detail.

As before, you have to write the plan first.

Once the plan is finished, return here and write the executive summary. It should be no longer than three paragraphs and should give just the main features of the business. It should be sober and sensible, not shouting or screaming with enthusiasm. The people who will read it have seen business plans come and go. They would not be impressed.

Now that we have started to think about writing, consider what style is best. My suggestion is that you:

- use a direct, clear type of English (which I am aiming for here);
- use short words and simple language;
- keep sentences short, one thought per sentence;
- keep paragraphs short, one argument per paragraph;
- use bullet-point lists when appropriate;

- make the main points well, but don't try to answer every potential question;
- number the pages;
- put any large mass of detail into an appendix, at the end.

Where people might want to refer in discussion to specific points, it helps if you number the relevant paragraphs or items in lists.

And when you have finished the plan, get someone who does not know the industry to read it, to see if it makes sense to them. Most official readers will not understand the industry either.

| The PLG Programme Section 1: Prepare | The PLG Programme Section 2: Launch | **The PLG Programme Section 3: Grow** |

Business Plan: Part one: Overviews

See: Chapter 13, *After a successful launch... developing your firm.*

Business overview

Here you describe what the business as a whole does and your vision for it. Imagine you are answering a bank manager who has asked: 'What is so special about this firm and what makes you think this idea will work?'

Your first bit of writing will say how it looks to you now, but as the plan evolves you will come here and change it. The headings of the plan follow:

Business background

Summarize only, giving notes on the main points. Bullet-points are fine.

Principals

Who you are – qualifications, background, experience.

Business history

How long you have been in business, financial and other performance in that time.

Present position

What is holding you back, how you want to develop.

Business identity

Legal constitution, business name, trading name. See: Chapter 5, *Your business name and legal status*.

Market background

See: Chapter 2, *Getting orders, making profits*.

The industry

The industry at present – structure, customers, suppliers, distribution system.

Unique proposition

Why customers come to you – the benefits you offer.

Market information

Market size, history and important issues.

Present suppliers

How customer needs are met by you and competitors, competitors and their methods and the share each holds (these can be estimated, in which case say so).

Market developments

What you expect to happen in future and how suppliers are likely to respond to your planned initiative.

The PLG Programme
Section 1: Prepare

The PLG Programme
Section 2: Launch

**The PLG Programme
Section 3: Grow**

Business plan: Part two: Operating plans

Marketing plans

Here you describe things in more detail. A balance needs to be struck between keeping it brief yet giving enough information. If tempted to write too much, remember you usually have a chance to answer questions face to face. In most cases you are asked to describe the current situation. See: Chapter 2, *Getting orders, making profits*.

Positioning

How your service or product is positioned against competition.

Sales proposition

Why the customer buys from you.

Target customers

Analyse the market, specify the group you aim at, say how many of them there are and where.

Pricing

Define your approach to pricing and relate it to your sales proposition.

Sales operations

How you contact and sell to customers, who does it, how many orders a week this produces and their value.

Promotion

How you support the sales effort and attract enquiries.

Distribution

By which channel(s) the product reaches the customer.

After-sales

Follow-up or opportunities to sell maintenance, etc.

Operating plans

See: Chapter 1, *First thoughts and foundations*; Chapter 2, *Getting orders, making profits*; Chapter 7, *Premises*; Chapter 8, *Managing operations*; Chapter 9, *Financial housekeeping, VAT and tax*; Chapter 10, *Employing people*; Chapter 11, *Risk management and insurance*.

Production

How what you plan to sell is to be produced, maximum output capacity and how it compares with sales forecasts, longer-term plans.

Premises

Plans for accommodation, how satisfactory it is, tenure, longer-term plans.

Administration

How you handle the admin of enquiries, orders, sales, invoices, accounts, stock, personnel.

Information systems

How stock is controlled, how accounting information for management is produced and when, how they will cope with growth.

IT

IT equipment and arrangements, who operates it, maintenance and support.

Sales forecast

Monthly for the first two years, annually for the next three.

Financial plans

This is part commentary, part tables. Tables for cash-flow forecasts, P&L forecasts and product costings are best set up on spreadsheets. That enables you to make the inevitable changes with the minimum of extra work. Your accountant should check your work first.

See: Chapter 3, *Controlling the money*; Chapter 4, *Raising the money*.

Capital requirements

The money needed to expand the business on a sound financial basis, divided into fixed capital (for long-term purchases) and working capital (to cover day-to-day fluctuations in cash flow).

Financing strategy

Where the money will come from, security offered, repayment period. If a limited company, how much in shares and how much on loan.

Cash-flow projection

Monthly, covering the first two years.

Profit-and-loss projection

Annually, covering the first five years.

The PLG Programme
Section 1: Prepare

The PLG Programme
Section 2: Launch

**The PLG Programme
Section 3: Grow**

Business plan: Part three: Appendices

An appendix is where you put the indigestible lumps of information that have to be present, but are too detailed or fussy for the main document, such as quotes for equipment. It is up to you to judge what to include or exclude here. The main document may refer to the appendix where necessary.

A CV for each of the principals in the firm is essential, and is best placed as an appendix. Detailed costings, historical accounts, copies of brochures and quotations for proposed purchases would all fit here too. Each appendix should be numbered.

Past accounts for the firm should also appear as appendices.

Business plan: Presentation

To make the best impression:

- Use white paper, selecting a font of 12pt (certainly no less than 10pt) for the main text.

- Don't use colour or fancy effects: they do not impress and they can delay or obstruct download if you send it as an e-mail attachment.

- Start with a title page, giving names, contact numbers and e-mail addresses and prominently featuring the word CONFIDENTIAL.

- Next, have a contents page.

- Check carefully for spelling and grammar; be sure that the different pieces are consistent with each other; have others read it to make sure it is quite clear.

- Put it in a cover that can easily be removed by the recipient for copying.

You have now completed your business plan for growth and the PLG Programme.

Congratulations, and best wishes for the future.

CASE STUDY Career change in the cantons

Danny's had a varied career as an entrepreneur. It's probably in his blood, as both parents and one set of grandparents were in business in Yorkshire. On moving to Switzerland with his new wife he started up International Collection Services GmbH. Charming and good-looking, he recognizes that a key strength is his sales skills. He was fascinated by the challenges of chasing people who had left a trail of unpaid debts behind them, often in countries around the world, and done their best to disappear. It was a moral as well as a commercial task: people have no right to break promises to pay, and when they do prices have to rise for others. Needless to say, he has a fund of stories – but that's not why he's featured here.

Danny analysed what it took to be the best in his line of business. First, competence: he concentrated on developing his skills; second, trustworthiness: he was absolutely straight with his clients, no spinning-out the process to increase his income at the client's expense; third, unrivalled personal service: keeping his clients informed at every step of the way.

The formula worked well for eight years but then other imperatives took over. He was spending too little time with his family, who are very important to him. The dilemma was that if he were to cut down his hours his service to clients would suffer – and the whole basis of the firm's existence would be undermined. After much deliberation, he decided that the family had to come first, and liquidated the firm.

So far, so good – more time with the family, yes, but his entrepreneurial juices were still flowing. Looking around for a new challenge, once again he did some analysis and brainstormed with a business partner. What did Switzerland have that draws people there from all over the world? Natural beauty and some of the cleanest air in the world. He couldn't can beauty, but the air is something that people living in suffocating cities would love to have. The Far East is home to many megalopolises where many people are wealthy but the air-quality is poor. They are rich enough to afford aerosols of Swiss mountain air to invigorate themselves after long days as salarymen in the stuffy, polluted, overcrowded cities, and there is a tradition in business of giving small gifts to customers and suppliers. From this, the new enterprise of Swiss Alpine Air GmbH, Edlibach, Switzerland was born. He acknowledges that there is much to learn about the sales and distribution process in China, and that costs at every stage need to be controlled, but his natural positiveness tells him he can deal with any challenge.

His words to an aspiring entrepreneur? I find them quite uplifting:

'If you don't try it, it won't happen. Listen to your heart, enjoy the ride and don't take things too seriously. There always seems to be a long line of people telling you it won't work. Don't listen to pessimists, pessimists have always failed before they start. Also note that many people who say it's a great idea are the people who will profit from your set-up (accountants, banks, suppliers etc.). Seek out like-minded people. Bask in the optimism of an entrepreneur, it is the most wonderful place to be.

'Your blind belief that it will work will be your success. Always keep overheads as low as possible. Surround yourself with successful people. Be brave, take risks but keep in touch with reality. Take a partner with you: it gets very lonely at times.'

dannywurr@gmail.com

APPENDIX 1
Cash-flow forecasting illustration

A simple example may help to explain the principles. John runs a very straightforward business selling apples from a market stall. On his first day in business he does the following:

- borrows £200 from his granny, interest-free, on the promise of repaying her as fast as possible;
- buys a market stall for £100 cash;
- pays the council £10 for a day's pitch on the market square;
- buys apples for £90 cash;
- sells half the apples for £80, all in cash.

At the end of that Monday his profit-and-loss account looks like Table A1.1.

Table A1.1 John's profit-and-loss account for Monday

	£
Sales	80
Cost of goods sold	45
Value added	35
Overheads	
Rent for pitch	10
Profit	25

But where are the £45-worth of apples he still has, and the stall worth £100? And for that matter, where is the £80 we know he has in his pocket? The answer is that the profit-and-loss account records only the sales, and the expenses relating to those sales. It could not show where stock, cash or equipment is. The 'missing' items will appear on the balance sheet, an entirely separate document. The balance sheet pretends that you stop all the buying and selling for a split second and record where money is tied up at that moment. It also shows where the money in the business has come from. At the end of Monday, John's balance sheet looks like Table A1.2.

Table A1.2   John's balance sheet

Where the money came from (liabilities)	£	Where it was at that moment (assets)	£
Loan from granny	200	Fixed assets (stall)	100
Retained profits	25	Current assets	
		Stock at cost (apples)	45
		Cash (day's takings)	80
	£225		£225

This way of showing a balance sheet is now old-fashioned, but it is easy to understand – so don't worry if balance sheets you have seen are laid out differently. They all mean the same thing.

You do not need to concern yourself further with balance sheets at this stage of your firm's development, so we shall leave them there. The point in mentioning them is so that you can see that they are basically simple documents, to illustrate the sort of information they contain and to confirm, yet again, that profit is only one of the two key matters you must deal with. Therefore, the young business needs to monitor its profit-and-loss account but need not worry about the balance sheet. Instead it pays hawk-like attention to its performance against the cash-flow forecast, which is a more flexible way of controlling and concentrating on the high-risk areas of the balance sheet.

To return to John. It is now Tuesday morning and he sets up his stall in the market again. He pays the council's superintendent another £10, and sells the rest of his apples for £80. The result of Tuesday's trading is shown in Table A1.3.

Table A1.3 John's profit-and-loss account for Tuesday

	£
Sales	80
Cost of goods sold	45
Value added	35
Overheads	
Rent of pitch	10
Profit	25

For the rest of the week he repeats the same pattern, ending up with profits of 6 × £25 = £150 by Saturday night, all in cash. Having made £150, and being a nice young chap, John thinks of paying off some of granny's loan. He knows he must keep some cash back to pay for stock on Monday, to pay the council, and to pay his mother his weekly keep. So he does a cash-flow forecast. He works out what cash he can expect to come in and when, and what he will have to pay out and when. Follow what John wrote down; even if it looks a little difficult at first it is not complicated. As usual, brackets mean a minus figure.

Table A1.4 shows that the result of Monday's trading is expected to be a fall of £50 in John's holding of cash, even though he will have made his usual profit. That profit, plus another £15, will be tied up in apples for sale on Tuesday. So can John pay off granny? Bearing in mind that he must start each day with enough cash for his outlays that day, he looks to see what he can pay granny and when. He will start week 2 with his £150 (the next to last figure in the Monday column) and he must finish the week with at least £130 for his outlays at the start of week 3. Try working out what he can pay, and when. The answer is in brackets below. If you found that a little challenging you will see why John did it on paper and not in

Table A1.4   John's cash-flow forecast for week 2 (£)

	Mon	**Tue**	**Wed**	**Thu**	**Fri**	**Sat**
Cash taken in day (a)	80	80	80	80	80	80
Cash paid out at start of day						
– keep	30	–	–	–	–	–
– rent	10	10	10	10	10	10
– apples	90	–	90	–	90	–
Total cash paid out in day (b)	130	10	100	10	100	10
Net cash taken in day (a – b)	(50)	70	(20)	70	(20)	70
Cash in hand at start of day	*150	100	170	150	220	200
Cash in hand at end of day	**100	170	150	220	200	270

* He will start the week with £150 left over from previous week.
** The figures on this line become the 'cash in hand at start of day' for the following day.

his head. The calculation is not difficult – it is only simple addition and subtraction – but there are so many steps to it that you cannot do it in your head. John could easily have taken the short cut and paid out of his profits. Had he done so he would have run out of cash and out of business. As it is, he still owes granny £60 but he is still in business.

(Answer: This week, John can pay £50 straight away, £20 on Monday evening, £50 on Wednesday evening, and £20 on Friday evening. If he tries to do it faster, he runs out of cash – so he still owes granny £60 at the end of the week. She won't mind – at this rate he'll have paid off the rest very soon.)

APPENDIX 2
Draft terms and conditions of sale

What follows is a list of suggestions. Some may be right for your business, others wrong, and some right after rewriting. Yet others may be needed that do not appear here. Use the list to build your own conditions of sale that reflect the way you want to deal with your customers. Then, and very importantly, *let your solicitor put it into proper shape.*

Terms and conditions of sale

Nothing in these terms and conditions should be seen as removing a customer's rights in law.

1   Descriptions shown in brochures, advertisements, on websites or other electronic media and by way of samples are correct at the time of going to press, errors and omissions excepted. They are liable to alteration at any time without notice.

    This is meant to protect you from minor complaints about changes in specification, and mistakes in website content price lists and catalogues. You might want to change a specification but not throw away catalogues. But it would not override the customer's legal right to goods that are 'fit for use'.

2   We may revise prices without notice. Prices will be those ruling at the date of dispatch. Any invoice query should be made in writing within 10 days of the date of the invoice. All prices exclude

VAT which is due at the rate currently in force. Quotations and estimates remain current for one month.

This is some protection against cost increases that you might have to pass on. This stops you being bound by old quotations and makes it clear that VAT has to be paid – if you are registered.

3   All accounts are payable in full within four weeks of invoice date.

Or whatever your terms are – very important to specify clearly.

4   We cannot accept liability for delay in dispatch or delivery.

It is not your fault if the delivery firm loses the parcel for a month.

5   Orders for goods may be cancelled only with the written agreement of one of our directors. Orders for goods made to special order cannot be cancelled.

Only a director or the owner should give this permission, not sales-people or others. Special orders are usually unsaleable to anyone else.

6   All orders over £100 will be delivered free within 10 miles. Elsewhere, carriage may be charged in addition to the quoted price. Orders for less than £100 are not normally accepted for a credit account.

Whether you charge for delivery and what you charge needs to be carefully controlled, as does the cost of administering a lot of small accounts. There is nothing special about £100; it is just an illustration.

7   Shortage of goods or damage must be notified by telephone within three days of delivery, and confirmed in writing within seven days of delivery, or no claim can be accepted. Delivery of obviously damaged goods should be refused. Notifications should give delivery note number, a list of quantities of the products damaged, and details of the type of damage. Damaged goods must be retained safely for inspection.

This should be written in the light of what your carrier's conditions say. As they will destroy all papers proving delivery after a short time, they want speedy notification of any claim. It is essential for damaged goods to be saved and eventually collected by you to stop dishonest collusion between customers and lorry drivers, and multiple claims against one damaged item. The mention of 'safe' storage is to ensure that goods are not left outside to be damaged to an extent that might make assessment of the original complaint difficult.

8 Liability cannot be accepted for non-delivery of goods if written notification is not received within 10 days of the date of invoice.

See comments on 7 above: tie in with carrier's conditions.

9 No liability is accepted for any consequential loss or damage whatsoever, however caused.

In cases of extreme negligence by your staff or yourself this would probably not stick, but your solicitor might want to see something like it included.

10 Acceptance of the goods implies acceptance of these conditions. These conditions may not be varied except in writing by one of our directors.

The customer cannot take the goods and then complain about the conditions. Nor can he or she bully your salesperson into giving unlimited credit, for instance.

11 Under some circumstances we may cancel the contract without notice or compensation. Such circumstances would include inability to obtain materials, labour and supplies, strikes, lockouts and other forms of industrial action or dispute, fire, flood, drought, weather conditions, war (whether declared or not), acts of terrorism, civil disturbance, acts of God or any other cause beyond our control making it impossible for us to fulfil the contract.

Cover for the times when snow blocks the roads and so on. You might even want to add the insurance policy favourites of damage by aircraft, falling trees, radioactive and biological hazards...but, there again, you might not.

12 Until they have been paid for we reserve our title in goods supplied.

When a customer goes into liquidation everything in his or her possession is sold to pay the creditors, even if it has not been paid for. The exceptions are items on lease or hire purchase, or that otherwise clearly belong to somebody else. You cannot normally snatch back the last delivery you sent. Clause 12 gives you protection, by saying that they remain yours until paid for. You could show the liquidator this term on the copy of the order form signed by the customer, and walk out with the goods. It will not work, however, if what you supplied has been incorporated in something else. Nor will it work if you cannot identify those items as precisely the ones on the invoice.

13 If an order is to be fulfilled in instalments, no instalment will be delivered until the previous instalment has been paid for.

14 Any invoice not paid in full by the due date shall attract interest payments. These will accrue from the due date at the rate of * * per cent per annum.

   * * The rate is calculated as eight per cent plus the 'reference rate', namely Bank of England base rate.

Unless you have a licence to offer credit you must not charge the public an interest rate. It is suggested that you think about using a clause like this to encourage payment in line with your terms. You would probably never need to actually charge it, as the threat would be enough to make most firms pay up. Any customer who queries it can be told that it does not apply to them, but only to people who break their promise to pay on time. **It is your legal right to do so.**

15 If a 'quotation' is given it is a firm price for the job but subject to these terms and conditions. An 'estimate' is our best estimate of the final cost but may be subject to fluctuation due to exigencies of the job which may be difficult or impossible to foresee.

In some businesses it is difficult to give a price for some work, as time may have to be spent to uncover the root of the problem before a proper quotation can be given. It is fair to the customer and yourself to make this clear.

APPENDIX 3
Small business contacts list

Neither author nor publisher can accept responsibility for the accuracy or content of websites, nor for advice given or withheld by these contacts, nor for the conduct of any organization mentioned.

Advisory, Conciliation and Arbitration Service (ACAS)
The Acas Helpline: 08457 47 47 47
www.acas.org.uk

British Franchise Association
01235 820470
www.thebfa.org

British Insurance Brokers Association
0344 770 0266
www.biba.org.uk

Building Research Establishment
0333 321 8811
www.bre.co.uk

Business Gateway (Scotland only)
0300 013 4753
www.bgateway.com

Business in the Community
020 7566 8650
www.bitc.org.uk

Chartered Institute of Marketing
01628 427120
www.cim.co.uk

Chartered Institute of Patent Attorneys
www.cipa.org.uk

Companies House
www.gov.uk/government/organisations/companies-house

Country Land and Business Association
020 7235 0511
www.cla.org.uk

Crafts Council
020 7806 2500
www.craftscouncil.org.uk

Department for Business
020 7215 5000
www.gov.uk/government/organisations/department-for-business-energy-and-industrial-strategy

Department for Communities and Local Government
0303 444 000
www.communities.gov.uk (for planning permission)

Department for International Trade
www.gov.uk/organisations/department-for-international-trade

Design Council
020 7420 5200
www.designcouncil.org.uk

Export Credits Guarantee Department
020 7271 8010
www.gov.uk/government/organisations/uk-export-finance

Federation of Small Businesses
0808 202 0888
www.fsb.org.uk

The Forum of Private Business
015 65 626 001
www.fpb.org

Greater London Enterprise
0800 032 0946
www.gle.co.uk

Highlands and Islands Enterprise
01463 245245
www.hie.co.uk

Institute of Directors
020 7451 3100
www.iod.com

Institute of Hospitality
www.instituteofhospitality.org

Institute of Patentees and Inventors
www.theipi.org.uk

Intellectual Property Office
0300 300 2000
www.gov.uk/government/organisations/intellectual-property-office

Invest Northern Ireland
0800 181 4422
www.investni.com

LiveWIRE – see Shell LiveWIRE

Manufacturers' Agents' Association of Great Britain and
01582 603439
www.themaa.co.uk

National Farmers' Union
024 7685 8500
www.nfuonline.com

The National Newspapers' Safe Home
Shopping Protection Scheme Ltd
01628 641930
www.shopspromise.com

Prince's Trust
0800 842 842
www.princes-trust.org.uk

Scottish Enterprise
0300 013 3385
www.scottish-enterprise.com

Shell LiveWIRE
0191 423 6229
www.shell-livewire.org

SHOPS (Safe Home Shopping Protection Scheme) – see The
National Newspapers' Safe Home Shopping Protection Scheme Ltd

The Stationery Office
0333 202 3070
www.tso.co.uk

Trade Marks Search
0300 300 2000
www.gov.uk/search-for-trade-mark

UK Business Angels' Association
020 7492 0490
www.ukbusinessangelsassociation.org.uk

Welsh Assembly Government business support
Tel: 0300 060 3000
www.businesswales.gov.wales

APPENDIX 4
Help for small businesses

The following organizations are some of those which offer help of various sorts for small firms.

- Banks. Most banks publish free booklets and offer advice on many aspects of starting and running a business, give away forms on which to do financial planning, and run newsletters.

- The Department for Business, Energy and Industrial Strategy help and advise on exporting

- Chambers of Commerce. Joining the local chamber can be a good way of making business contacts, as well as giving you access to a library and information service, help with exporting, and a voice in representations to public authorities.

- Chambers of Trade. Quite separate from Chambers of Commerce, which usually serve industry and commerce, Chambers of Trade do similar work for retailers and wholesalers.

- Cooperative development agencies. These organizations give help and advice to people wishing to set up a cooperative venture.

- County courts. They give information on making claims for payment of debts, and what to do if such a claim is made against you.

- Department for Business, Energy and Industrial Strategy. This government department is the main source of grants for industry. Its regional offices can advise on every facet of their help (visit **www.gov.uk**).

- Local enterprise partnerships. These partnerships between the public and private sectors aim to offer advice, help and other facilities to encourage new and existing businesses.

- Highlands and Islands Enterprise. This northern Scottish organization supports, helps and promotes small businesses in its area.

- HM Revenue & Customs Inspectors of Taxes. Leaflets and advice are given on the tax position of businesses, which can be most useful to new starters (visit **www.hmrc.gov.uk**).

- HM Revenue & Customs VAT offices. Their staff offer advice on all aspects of VAT and dispense free booklets (visit **www.gov.uk/hmrc**).

- Intellectual Property Office. The Intellectual Property Office offers information on trademarks, registered designs and patents.

- Jobcentres. Not only are they a source of recruitment, but Jobcentres also carry a stock of leaflets and Department for Work and Pensions publications, many of which are essential reading for an employer.

- Local authorities. They can usually provide information on any industrial aid which may be available locally. In addition, as one of the most influential enforcement bodies acting on small firms, they can advise you on how to avoid trouble. The main contacts are the planning department, health inspectors, the fire department, building inspectors (who are now mostly contracted out) and trading standards offices.

- Newspaper Publishers Association. This body lays down the rules governing, among other things, mail-order advertising in most newspapers and magazines. Anyone planning to sell by this method should contact them well in advance of trying to advertise.

- Royal Mail. The Royal Mail gives considerable concessions to volume users of its services in general, and especially to first-time users of direct-mail selling.

- Tourist Boards. Organized regionally, the Tourist Boards offer management advice and publicity to their tourism-based members. These do not have to be just hotels: they are concerned to help most firms having some tourism aspect to their operations. They also publish some useful guides to running different sorts of tourism businesses.

APPENDIX 5
Taking up a franchise

Overview

As mentioned earlier, this way of getting into business has special characteristics all of its own. There are many models of franchising, but what is most often meant is the 'business format' franchise. This is where a franchisor, including such well-known names as Prontaprint, Burger King and Holiday Inn, invites you to run your own business as a franchisee under their trading name. The customers think that you are simply the local branch, but you are, in fact, an independent business.

As a franchisee, though, independence does have its limits. You operate under a formal agreement for a given period of time and are expected to conform to a lengthy and detailed specification of how the business is run and presented. In return for the short cut into an established business formula, you hand over not only a lot of your independence but also up-front fees and continuing royalties based on sales or profitability.

Equally, in taking up a well-established and well-run franchise, you become part of a business family in which everyone wants you to succeed. That does not relieve you of the responsibility to run your operation effectively – franchises do not guarantee success – but it is something that certain types of people value. Just as, in families, dad is likely to take an interest in the state of the teenagers' bedrooms and makes a considerable fuss if they are untidy, a franchisor has a keen concern for the way each of its 'branches' is run. Consequently, part of the agreement is that you will be subject to inspection by the franchisor to see if its standards are being met, and will be given feedback on its findings. Thus franchising is not for the person who becomes prickly in the face of criticism. The way to see this is not as an unwarranted infringement of your right to run your firm as you wish (you signed that away when you signed the franchise agreement) but as an objective view by people who know more about the business than you do, aimed at helping you improve. Not all teenagers see parental attitudes in that way but, once they are parents themselves, they realize that dad really does know better.

Is a franchise really for me?

The panel below shows a simplified comparison between running one's own show and running a franchise. From this analysis, it may look as if a franchise is for the faint-hearted, appealing to the person who is unsure of their judgment and who is uncomfortable at taking sole responsibility for a new enterprise. That probably describes about 80 per cent of the readership of this book, but it does not mean that they should all fly to the apparent comfort of franchises. Rather, it reflects the fact that, at the planning stage of a new business, it is a rash person who has complete and unconditional confidence.

Darwin might be a useful guide at this point. Our cave-dwelling ancestors were divided into those who looked both ways before stepping out into new terrain, constantly on the alert for dangers, and those who went ahead thoughtlessly, confident in their ability to meet any problem. We who are alive today are descended from the first group and thus share some of their characteristics. The second group rarely lived long enough to reproduce, so their strain largely died out.

Thus it is only natural to temper confidence with a little fear at this early stage, but that fear should be kept under control and used

Table A5.1 Franchising vs your own operation

	Your own operation	Franchise
Business idea	You devise	Ready-made
Prior understanding	High need	Lower need
Business formula	You devise	Ready-made
Supply sources	You specify	They specify
Finance	You specify and find	They specify, you find
Continuing support	You find	They supply some
Certainty of success	Variable	Less variable
Potential returns	Infinite	Limited

not to forbid initiative but rather to spur us to look ahead to possible risks and assess them soberly. How can we best use that anxiety in the context of franchises?

One thing a franchise cannot eliminate is the self-employed workload. Unlike an employee, and just like anyone who is self-employed you are in, effect, doing several jobs, each of which takes time. It might reduce some aspects of the workload, for example in planning your advertising and promotion, but that will probably be made up for by the need to ensure that for every minute of the working day you, your staff and your premises meet the exacting demands of the franchise operator. For somewhere in your franchise agreement will be a clause entitling the franchise operator to check up on you, and if you misbehave badly enough or often enough, to cancel the franchise and put you out of business.

Selecting a franchise

The obvious course is to seek one that reflects your own experience and abilities. If your selection also ticks other boxes (for affordability, credibility, experience, etc) you might need to look no further. On the other hand, there may be opportunities that do not match the profile of your personal experience but which you could run successfully.

These different approaches may be useful (they are in no special order):

- don't take up a franchise, but look at those on offer in your chosen field to see if their formula is worth copying but with your own special twist;

- look at the franchises on offer outside your chosen field; identify ideas that can be imported into your own field or business, or even discover an entirely new business idea you could pursue;

- identify your personal shortcomings in relation to the firm you plan to start and the problems you foresee. Can you overcome them? If not, would a franchise remove them?

If after all this you decide that a franchise would be right for you, before looking seriously at any franchise proposition, it may pay to contact the British Franchise Association (BFA): **www.thebfa. org**. The BFA represents nearly half of the franchisors in the United Kingdom; members are required to sign up to a code of ethics and pay a hefty annual membership fee (nearly £5,000 for the largest). The BFA advises careful research at every stage, and taking decisions only at the pace that suits you, not someone else. The six common-sense steps that they urge are:

1 Using a BFA member (no surprise there, you may think).

2 Making sure you can afford the investment and that it will pay you enough.

3 Making an honest assessment of yourself, your capacities and your requirements.

4 Researching the markets within which your shortlisted franchises operate.

5 Researching the franchise itself.

6 Taking professional advice

7 Taking time and getting advice to get the decision right.

Their website gives a lot of information on general matters as well as a brief description of members' activities and links to their websites. Members cover a surprising range of activity, from hi-fi showrooms to pet boarding. The BFA has also had a legal expert prepare a list of 50 questions to put to any organization offering franchises.

Despite all the glossy brochures and persuasive sales-talk, the people offering franchises are only human, and therefore capable of making catastrophic mistakes in the future running of their brand. (Some might even be crooks, but by dealing only with BFA members you would expect to have some protection.) That said, the greatest risk that a business runs is in its first five years, when around a third fail. After that, the failure-rate drops dramatically, to about 10 per cent a year – still high, but not as bad as at the outset. Since most franchises are more than five years of age (and be wary of one that is not), that early high-risk period has passed. That said, it doesn't pay to get too depressed – after all, 70 per cent of firms survive their first five years, and 90 per cent every year afterwards.

The issues to address when selecting a franchise include:

- the product or service itself: you must be happy working in the field concerned;

- the area covered: is it big enough, does it have enough potential, is the competition not too fierce, if it is bricks and mortor-based are you also allowed to trade on the internet (and are other holders of the same franchise allowed to too)?;

- how you and the franchisor fit together: are they too demanding, do they offer enough support, are other franchisees happy, do they give fully satisfactory answers to your questions?;

- track record: is the package proven in the country you plan to operate in (some overseas, especially American, franchisors assume that their package works universally – don't be the one who proves them wrong, at your expense), how many previous holders have dropped out, and why?;

- finance: can you afford the initial outlay, what happens to your profits if their sales forecasts are too high?

No list given here can cover all the ground required by a proper assessment.

Conclusion

Thus franchising may seem, in principle, to offer a lower-risk way of getting into business, but there is a price to be paid, via limits to your freedom of action and in the fees to be met. Equally, by investigating franchises you may find examples to be copied and improved on by your own firm. For the more cautious entrepreneur, a few years learning the ropes as a franchisee could precede starting out on your own, though note that the franchise agreement is likely to forbid starting up a directly competing business. Alternatively, if you are more impatient, you might learn a lot by finding a job with a franchisee – even unpaid – to understand how the business works and if it feels right for you.

APPENDIX 6
Starting a green business

Why a green business?

Successive governments, as well as the UN, have emphasized the urgent need for the human race to clean up its act. In the 19th century a reaction took place to industry pouring its waste into rivers, lakes and the air and despoiling the environment for all. During the 20th century practical action ensured that rivers were cleaner and that the poisonous smogs became a thing of the past. Rose-growers lament the cleaning-up of the atmosphere, as the fungal disease black spot is now rampant: formerly air-borne SO_2 killed it off, but most would agree that their distress is a price worth paying to keep forests alive.

Now the great drive is to reduce man-made atmospheric CO_2, in the belief that it is causing an unprecedented and potentially catastrophic warming of the planet. Governments are pouring in, or at least promising to pour in, vast sums of taxpayers' money to help industry to adjust, and taxing those activities seen as socially undesirable. Hand-in-hand with that runs an entirely reasonable pressure to reduce waste in all its forms: putting reusable materials into holes in the ground itself costs money, as well as ignoring a chance to recycle. The general public seems largely to have been convinced that something must be done and many are cheerfully paying over the odds for purchases that appear to be green.

Times of great social, scientific or economic change throw up new opportunities for entrepreneurs. The environmental revolution represents one of those times. Ten years from now the opportunities will seem obvious, for the businesses formed today will have established themselves and grown. Today they are less obvious, but the chances are there nonetheless.

The opportunity is therefore clear: a business that either helps others to reduce their carbon footprint or waste, or in its own operations can demonstrate lower carbon use and waste than its competitors, should thrive. Less idealistically, a firm that wishes to supply large companies may find itself locked out if it does not possess, or is not working towards, certification of its environmental management system.

Why not a green business?

The wrong motive is to be attracted by any subsidies on offer. Any business that depends for its existence on government handouts relies on a variable income which can be withdrawn at any time and can be a nightmare to negotiate. That does not rule out their use, but suggests that no long-term commitments should be made on the assumption of that income continuing.

The evidence on which belief in man-made climate change is based is constantly under scrutiny, though the sceptics appear to have lost the fight, at least in most government circles. If the pendulum should swing back, much of the impetus towards greenness may evaporate. Meanwhile, and perhaps permanently, greenness can be a powerful promotional tool.

What is a green business?

The main ways of being commercially green include:

- running a conventional firm, but using fewer resources than is usual in that trade or industry;

- developing ways of encouraging or facilitating reuse or recycling rather than disposal;

- helping others to use fewer resources, through consultancy or ideas;

- inventing products or processes that will increase the efficiency of other businesses;

- inventing new, greener products that supersede existing products.

The spectrum covered by that list is enormous. At one end is the guest house that improves its heat insulation and sources as many of its purchases as possible locally, thus cutting down the energy required for deliveries and heating. At another is the engineer who develops a way to capture and store underground the carbon emissions of coal-fired power stations.

There is a further dimension: certification. If a business is to argue that its operations are green, it might decide to try to get away with no more than the fuzzy statement that they are. It might think that all it needs to do to support it is take a few token measures – a windmill on the roof, a solar panel or two dotted around and a hybrid car in the car park. In dealing with undemanding customers among the general public that may be all that is required to convince. However, some buyers are rather more hard-headed, demanding evidence of compliance with written standards. Typically they are in large-scale industry.

Examining the standards that exist means entering a world of alphabet soup: British Standard (BS) 8555:2003 Environmental Management System, or to give it the full title, 'Guide to the phased implementation of an environmental management system including the use of environmental performance evaluation', links Environmental Management Systems (ISO 14001) and Environmental Performance Evaluation (ISO 14031). Nobody should be under any illusion about the challenge of conforming to the requirements of a major certification scheme at the same time as trying to set up a business, although some BSI schemes are designed specifically for SMEs.

Where are the opportunities?

The key tool is the Pareto analysis (discussed earlier), which helps to identify where the big offenders are – the big offenders are those that offer the greatest chance of a big saving in waste or carbon footprint, which will also be keen to reduce it, and are therefore worth concentrating on.

For example, most people, asked who are the greatest producers of atmospheric carbon might answer 'motor vehicles' or 'aircraft'. They would completely overlook shipping, which accounts for around twice aviation's quantity. Only research and a close inspection of the figures would reveal information like that, so an investigation of the facts might lead to all kinds of new perspectives on the opportunities available.

Consistency – can you keep it up?

Anyone who runs a green firm needs to be a believer; anyone else would not be able to stop the mask from slipping. They need to have, and stick to, green policies on every aspect of their firm's operations; for those in a certification scheme, procedures will all be laid down. For those who are not, here's a checklist:

- premises: heating, lighting;
- travel to work: minimize the use of motor vehicles, possibly by working from home when possible;
- staff: live locally, preferably walk or cycle to work;
- meetings: face-to-face locally, video or phone conferencing remotely, wherever possible;
- business travel: public transport wherever possible, minimizing driving, shipping and flying;
- business accommodation when travelling: environmentally responsible hotels;
- motor vehicles: as few as possible, and the most environmentally responsible available, irrespective of comfort, etc;
- services and consumables: bought locally, from suppliers who themselves source locally;
- equipment: should have the best environmental performance;
- product or service design and delivery: maximum resource efficiency;
- waste: minimized, but where unavoidable, reuseable or recyclable.

To keep to that list you would need really to be convinced and, moreover, would need to persuade your staff to adopt a similar level of commitment. Anyone who was less than convinced would inevitably show their hand at some point and possibly harm your reputation, perhaps catastrophically. On the other hand, staff with green convictions are likely to be highly motivated to work effectively for the cause.

Summary

Before following this track much thought is needed. In particular, consider:

- whether you really are green, and define the firm as green only if the answer is a resounding 'yes';
- the need for much research into what is going on, constantly looking for green opportunities;
- the fact that 'green' is much more than just a promotional sticker to add to a conventional firm; it is more a way of life that has to be lived 24/7;
- whether or not your likely customers will demand membership of a certification scheme.

INDEX

CPSIA information can be obtained
at www.ICGtesting.com
Printed in the USA
LVOW13s2357210518
578043I.V00030B/935/P